Copyright © 2023, Emilee Avink

All rights reserved. This book or any portion thereof may not be reproduced or used in any manner whatsoever without the express written permission of the author except for the use of brief quotations in a book review.

Printed by LuLu POD, Inc. in the United States of America

First POD, 2023.

https://naturesauracrystals.com/

Table of Contents:

Hello, curious ones! I am thrilled to share my first book with you, "Embracing the Witches Shadow: A Guide to Transformation and Self-Discovery. Throughout these pages, you will discover a journey of introspection and soul-searching no other can rival. Being a witch, I have been drawn to shadows by nature; the shadow within us that we always try and avoid. Yet it is those shadows of our humanness that contain some greatest forces for magic and transformation. So, with this book I am inviting you to go on an adventure of self-discovery, where you'll will plunge into the depths of your soul to seek out and empower your magick. Light your candles, call a circle and you'll begin your trip.

This Book is Dedicated to the Seekers of Inner Light.

For the brave who wish to know,

To the courageous ones who dare to tread into darkness,

Here is to a trip of radical change.

And may your findings shed light on the road to self-understanding.

This book is your companion as you embark on the mystical journey of shadow work,

Uncovering the hidden sides of your soul,

It is discovering your true self in the darkness of night.

The Witch's Shadow calls to you. Go ahead and take it in your begin, get ready for the inevitable manifestation of magic that will occur inside once you do so!

I would like your journey through the book to bring the realization, development and great transformation in you as you enter into shadow self aspects of yours which can play a very powerful role in your life and your witchcraft practices.

Chapter 1

Introduction to Witches Shadow Work

In that regard, shadow work is one significant aspect of contemporary witchcraft and involves an introspective exercise in self-awareness. It requires diving into the secret bottoms of your subconscious, facing deep-seated phobias and surpressed feelings that need to be resolved. Though the very name of shadow work might seem scary, it is a valuable instrument that no witch can ignore on their journey towards self development and independence.

The shadow is a that part of you which so much gets neglected or what people always try to leave out in their everyday lives. These are the aspects of who you really, society culture upbringing or even your irrational fears have taught us to bury. Shadow work has its roots in the teachings of famous psychologist Carl Jung, who insisted that acknowledging your shadows is a prerequisite to attaining personal growth. Within the shadow work of a witch, Jung teaches about various archetypes that are essential to understand how human's psyches possess multi-pronged complexities. The next twelve most famous, as they analyze above higher level of knowledges about particular archetypes that makes significant contributions to this journey for development.

-The Hero: Represents the aspirational aspect, inspiring individuals to face challenges within their shadow. Embracing the hero archetype involves courageously confronting and overcoming deep-seated fears.

-The Shadow: This archetype embodies the hidden, darker elements within the self. Acknowledging and integrating the shadow is key to achieving harmony and self-awareness.

-The Anima/Animus: Symbolizes the feminine (anima) or masculine (animus) aspects within individuals. To explore these archetypes fosters a deeper understanding of one's gendered and emotional complexities.

-The Wise Old Man/Woman: Represents wisdom and guidance. Connecting with this archetype involves seeking inner wisdom to navigate the complexities of the shadow and its integration.

-The Trickster: Personifies unpredictability and mischief. Engaging with the trickster archetype invites individuals to embrace the playful and unpredictable aspects of their shadow, fostering adaptability.

-The Mother: Embodies nurturing and protective qualities. Exploring the mother archetype involves understanding one's relationship with nurturing and how it influences the shadow's expression.

-The Child: Symbolizes innocence and spontaneity. Connecting with the child archetype allows individuals to explore the untainted aspects of their shadow, fostering creativity and curiosity.

-The Lover: Represents passion and emotional connection. Engaging with the lover archetype involves exploring the emotional aspects of the shadow and embracing passion in its various forms.

-The Magician: Embodies transformative power and intuition. Connecting with the magician archetype involves tapping into one's innate ability to bring about change and transformation within the shadow.

-The Ruler: Symbolizes order and control. Exploring the ruler archetype involves understanding one's relationship with control and authority within the shadow.

-The Sage: Personifies knowledge and reflection. Engaging with the sage archetype invites individuals to explore their intellectual and introspective facets within the shadow.

-The Jester: Represents humor and lightheartedness. Connecting with the jester archetype involves embracing the lighter side of the shadow and finding joy in the midst of self-exploration.

Understanding and integrating these archetypes provides a thorough structure for navigating the elaborate geography of witch's shadow work. Each archetype contributes unmatched insights, promoting an extensive and life-changing journey towards personal growth.

Courageously facing and embracing your own shadows will channel the might of personal power as well as spiritual enlightenment. This process helps you to comprehend and own traumas, insecurities and fears of yours so that these become sources power and insight. Therefore, this works as a catalyst for self-empowering and realizing your full capacity. By accepting and owning your shadows, you can achieve balance and embrace the force that makes one more potent in their craft hence able to overcome life's obstacles with wisdom.

In this book, you'll initiate a quest to explore the dimensions of shadow work and it's use in witchcraft. You'll get into the many facets of your inner self and uncover the enchantment within your depths. The deeper your exploration into shadow work, the clearer it will become that embracing your shadows and diving into the darkness is not merely a means of self-empowerment. It evolves into a strong manifestation of self-love, revealing the acknowledgement and integrating all aspects of your inner self. It is in these shadows that you discover the essence of your true self and find the keys to unlocking your potential as a witch. Through the pages that follow, you will unravel the mystique of shadow work and ultimately realizing that our shadows are not adversaries but allies on this sacred path.

Chapter 2

Witch's Shadow Work Essentials

Shadow work is a way of understanding that awakens through diving into the depths of your mind. These include symbolic tools and materials that help to reinforce this practice with a greater spiritual connection for you but the most critical are in your own hand.

Crystals

As you start on the path of shadow work, crystals make for excellent allies to help with your journey. For instance, amethyst's soothing nature can guide you to face and process your deeply rooted emotions. Labradorite has been shown to stimulate intuition and increase self-awareness, which is essential for shadow work. Obsidian is excellent for grounding and protection purposes, while smoky quartz assists in releasing negative energy. By responding to these crystals by carrying and meditating with them, you allow their energies into your reality so that they would be able to contribute towards more of a transfiguration environment during the duration where inward contemplation takes place.

The book of Crystal Magick by Judy Ann Nock is fascinating with a detailed analysis of the origins and power of crystals from ancient times to practical modern spells. With its diverse collection of crystals—still resonant through the mists of history, now medleyed into fresh magical designs—this exquisite book lightly lifts the veil off to reveal not only new facets within but also reborn energies that are fertile for vibrancy and promise in ritual use. The intricate guide on using crystals and how to choose them will not only make the reader's comprehension relating to this field better but also becomes a precious asset in unveiling the hidden beauty, potency, and knowledge of Mother Earth's magick.

My beloved crystals are my helpers, comforting me during meditation. The carving of a selenite heart is small but powerful with soothing energies that favor mental stillness and a sereneness inside. Prophet Stone helps in receiving special revelations and inspires great insights or high intuition when used as a guide through my spiritual journeys. Smokey Quartz helps to neutralize negativity while instilling within us the qualities of balance and calmness. Finally, my Angel Aura Clear Quartz tower has celestial vibrations that boost my spiritual connections thus taking my meditation practices a notch higher.

Herbs

Herbal magic holds an important key to amplifying dreams and forging a profound connection with the subconscious. Mugwort, famed for its dream-improving qualities, and wormwood, regularly related to psychic development, provide pathways to delve into the depths of the psyche in the course of sleep. Utilizing those herbs in sachets, teas, or as integral elements for your sacred space infuses your exercise with their mighty energies, fostering a richer dream revel in and a deeper expertise of the internal self.

Rosemary, with its purifying aroma, serves as an best friend in creating a sanctified environment conducive to shadow work. This herb contributes to cleaning sacred spaces, placing the degree for introspective trips. Whether incorporated into teas, sachets, or as an fragrance for your sacred space, rosemary becomes a beacon for purification. In the pursuit of herbal knowledge, the book "Herbal Tea Magic for the Modern Witch"; by Elsie Wild serves as an insightful guide, supplying treasured insights into the artwork of natural tea crafting for magical and healing practices.

As you embark on an herbal magic adventure, it is important to prioritize protection while consuming herbs, verifying their safety for consumption before incorporating them into teas or other rituals in which you would ingest the herbs. This ensures a harmonious blend of magical practices and safety.

Tarot or Oracle Cards

Tarot cards are powerful tools for diving into the depths of self-reflection and insight. Each card in the deck carries symbolic significance, making them ideal to use. The Death card, with its symbolism of transformation and rebirth, invites you to embrace change and growth. The Moon card, representing the exploration of the subconscious, aids in uncovering hidden truths and navigating the intricacies of the inner self. Additionally, the High Priestess, symbolizing intuition and inner wisdom, guides you through your journey, providing valuable insights into the hidden aspects of your psyche.

Oracle cards function as priceless tools for witches, presenting a unique and customized mode for self-discovery. These decks often depict symbols, archetypes, and subject matters deeply rooted in witchcraft, allowing you to discover the hidden realms of your subconscious throught a magical lens. The symbolism within oracle cards resonates with the magical components of the craft, facilitating a deeper connection to the energies at play at some stage in your shadow work. Whether it is the enchanting imagery of black cats, witches, or mythic landscapes, these oracle cards function as mirrors reflecting your internal horizon. The interpretative nature of oracle cards lets you tap into your intuition and draw insights from the magical symbolism.

An excellent resource for digging deeper into the complexities of tarot and its application in shadow work is "78 Degrees of Wisdom" by Rachel Pollack. Pollack's meticulous explanations of each card, whether in an upright or reversed position, offer a rich tapestry of symbolism and meaning. Her expertise enhances understanding, making the book a fundamental guide for those seeking a comprehensive exploration of tarot's symbolism and its application in various aspects of personal and spiritual development.

Candles

Candles play a considerable part in spiritual practices, specifically within the meaning of shadow work, in which they may be utilized to symbolize and facilitate illumination and transformation. Black candles maintain a deep symbolic meaning, the representation of the mysteries living in your unconscious mind. The shade black is frequently related to the unknown, inviting you to delve into the depths in their psyche and confront hidden components of the self. On the opposite hand, white candles embody purity and clarity, serving as a beacon to light up the course toward self-attention and understanding.

The choice of candle colors in shadow work isn't arbitrary; it carries symbolic significance deeply rooted in the psychology of colors. Black, as a color associated with mystery and the unknown, aligns with the depth of the unconscious mind. White, representing purity and clarity, serves as a beacon to illuminate the hidden recesses, fostering self-awareness and understanding. When engaging in shadow work, the ritual act of lighting a candle transcends the physical realm. It becomes a dynamic and intentional practice, a sacred gesture that focuses one's intentions and creates an atmosphere conducive to self-exploration. This ritualistic use of candles enhances the spiritual experience, providing a tangible and symbolic guide through the complexities of the inner self.

As the candle flame flickers, it not only illuminates your physical space but also acts as a metaphor for the internal journey. The dance of light and shadow becomes a visual representation of the emotional and psychological processes occurring within. This dynamic interplay of energies, channeled through the ritual of candle lighting, transforms the practice of shadow work into a sacred exploration, inviting you to confront, embrace, and integrate all facets of your being.

Journal

Engaging in the practice of journaling is not only essential but transformative in your shadow work journey. This intentional act gives you a sacred space to document the complex layers of your thoughts, dreams, and observations as you move through the depths of your inner self. The act of putting pen to paper or writing down your thoughts serves as a powerful means of expressing and processing the nuances of your emotions, allowing you to unravel the complexities within your psyche.

Journaling serves as a dynamic tool for self-reflection and growth. By recording your experiences and insights, you create a tangible record that allows you to track your progress over time. This reflective practice uncovers patterns, triggers, and recurring themes in your journey and offers valuable insights into your personal expansion. Your journal becomes a repository of wisdom, capturing lessons learned and an evolving understanding of yourself.

Beyond just being a record, your journal will develop into a sacred archive of your experiences. It becomes a testament to your courage and commitment to self-discovery. The pages bear witness to your vulnerability, your resilience, and the profound transformations that take place within. Returning to these written reflections can be a source of inspiration, offering a tangible reminder of your growth and encouraging you to persevere on your journey of introspection and personal development.

Chapter 3

Crafting the Sacred Realm

The need to build a sacred space for shadow work involves providing an area where the energies align, which would help to bring reflection. An environment of your choice, free of clutter and noise, becomes a vessel through which questions that are innately personal to you can begin to examine your soul. Cleansing rituals with spiritually charged tools ensure that the space is ready, free of any obstructive or negative energies. An altar adorned with objects that can be perceived as personally meaningful objects then becomes a representation of the intentions of the work, ultimately facilitating a grounded or marked connection. What I've learned in my practice is that doing shadow work in this sacred space amplifies concentration and spiritual resonance and provides a much more focused bubble of pristine energy than practicing anywhere else. When you're finished what you have is a deliberately designed space that enhances the deep shadow work; this supports an authentic path of transformation.

-Choose a Quiet Place

Choosing the right location for your shadow work is essential to creating an environment conducive to deep introspection and self-discovery. In addition to practical considerations, such as ensuring freedom from distractions and noise, it is essential to align with the energetic qualities of the chosen space. Find a place that resonates with a calming and harmonious atmosphere, as the energy of the surroundings can significantly affect the effectiveness of your shadowwork practice. This can manifest as a cozy corner in your bedroom where you can hide in comfort and introspection. Alternatively, a secluded location in nature offers the added benefit of connecting with the grounding energy of the outdoors, enhancing the transformative nature of your shadow work. If nature is not readily available, a quiet room in your home, thoughtfully designed to promote a peaceful atmosphere, can serve as an ideal retreat for focused, uninterrupted shadow exploration.

-Cleansing Ritual

Cleansing your space is a holistic practice, encompassing both physical and spiritual dimensions. The careful selection of cleansing tools, such as cedar, bay leaf, or incense, holds profound significance, each carrying its own spiritual energy. Utilizing these tools in your cleansing ritual goes beyond mere physical purification; it serves to dispel negative or stagnant energies, creating a harmonious environment conducive to effective shadow work. As witches, the conscientious consideration of materials and methods is paramount. Opting for alternatives like common garden sage, rather than white sage, becomes not only a responsible choice but a vital step in demonstrating respect for indigenous cultures, as white sage is also employed in parts of Mexico. Mindful practices safeguard against cultural appropriation, ensuring that our rituals contribute positively to the spiritual landscape without causing harm or offense to the communities we seek to honor.

-Altar or Focus Point: Your altar or focal point is a visual representation of your intentions. The objects you choose should have personal meaning and significance. Personal items that you might consider adding to your altar include things like photographs of loved ones, items from nature such as feathers or stones, crystals, candles, a journal for recording your thoughts and reflections, symbols representing your spiritual or religious beliefs, and any other objects that hold personal significance to you. It's important to choose items that resonate with your intentions and that help you feel grounded and connected during your practice.

-Meditation and Visualization: Incorporating meditation and visualization practices in your sacred space can be a great way to connect with your inner self. These techniques can help you relax, set intentions, and create a mindset that is conducive to shadow work. Remember to make your sacred space a comfortable and inviting environment where you can fully immerse yourself in these practices. To incorporate visualization and meditation in your sacred space, you might consider lighting candles, burning incense, and creating a calming atmosphere. You could also try visualizing a calm and peaceful environment, or meditating on a specific intention or emotion you wish to explore. You may choose to visualize a safe and protective aura around your space or meditate on your shadow self to better understand it.

-Protection and Boundaries: When you're engaging in shadow work, it's important to establish clear boundaries and protection for your well-being. Certain crystals, such as black tourmaline and amethyst, can be helpful in providing protection, while symbols like the pentacle can act as a barrier. By creating a safe space for yourself, you can ensure that the energy you're working with stays contained and prevent any unwanted interference from external forces during your shadow work process.

Chapter 4

Safeguarding the Circle: Boundary Spell for Protection

Shadow work is a compelling tool that involves confronting and learning from your suppressed emotions and fears. It's a deeply reflective development that requires you to establish a protective barrier around yourself. This boundary spell is crucial not only for your safety but also for safeguarding the sanctity of the inner expedition.

This spell creates a protective circle, serving as a barrier against any external influences. During shadow work, you may encounter intense and unsettling emotions or memories. This spell acts as a shield, preventing any unwanted or negative forces from interfering with the your inner exploration.

The boundary spell enhances the your confidence and courage. Knowing that a protective circle is in place can provide a sense of security, enables you to approach your shadow self with more resilience and self-assurance. It's a reminder that, no matter how challenging this process may become, you are in control of your space and can confront your shadow self with fortitude.

You Will Need:

- **A black candle:** The black candle symbolizes protection and banishing negativity.

- **A bowl of salt:** Salt is renowned for its purifying properties in many spiritual practices.

- **A small bowl of water:** Water is a symbol of emotions and purification.

- **A feather or incense for air representation:** Including this element ensures that your thoughts are clear, and your communication with your shadow self is unobstructed.

- **A small stone or crystal for earth representation:** This grounding ensures stability and strength, providing a solid foundation for your emotional and spiritual exploration during the shadow work.

- **A white candle:** It also acts as a symbol of your own inner light, reminding you that, even in the shadows, you possess the power to confront and transform. Also represents the fire element, when lit.

Steps:

1. Begin by setting up your ritual space, ensuring that you won't be disturbed. Light the white candle to symbolize purification and light.

2. Stand in the center of your space, take a few deep breaths to center yourself, and ground your energy.

3. Light the black candle, representing protection. Hold it in your hands, and visualize a sphere of protective light forming around you.

4. With the black candle, move clockwise around your ritual space, sprinkling a circle of salt to define the boundary. **(If you are performing this spell outside, please do not use salt for your circle, instead choose an herb that won't hurt the earth.)** As you do this, envision a protective golden light forming around you.

5. Place the salt (or herbs) bowl at the entrance to your circle as a physical representation of your protective boundary.

6. Move to the east of your circle, and with the feather or incense, trace the symbol of air in the air, invoking the energy of clear thought and protection.

7. Move to the south, and with the stone or crystal, trace the symbol of earth on the ground, invoking the energy of stability and grounding.

8. Move to the west, and with your fingers, sprinkle a few drops of water in the symbol of water, invoking emotional protection.

9. Finally, move to the north, and hold your hands to your heart, visualizing a protective shield of glowing light enveloping your circle.

10. Stand in the center of your circle, close your eyes, and focus on your intention: "I am protected, and my shadow work is done in safety and empowerment."

11. When you feel the protective energy is strong, extinguish the black candle. Your protective boundary is now in place.

12. Begin your shadow work within the sacred and protected space, knowing that you are shielded from any negative energies during your exploration. Remember to blow out the white candle once you are done with your ritual to ensure fire safety. Remember to close your circle and release the boundary when your shadow work is complete.

Chapter 5

Invoking the Magick Within with Affirmations

The more you get involved in these pages, the more wisdom will become your guiding light showing you the path of self-analysis and self-development. While on this spiritual journey, this book serves as your guide and companion that provides valuable information to help you understand both dark and light aspects of your being.

From here, you gently wander into the charming world of affirmations. These affirmations are not mere words but indeed powerful spells that nourish love for self and self-empowerment. Within the daily recitation of these affirmations, you will encounter captivating expressions that enlighten you to your inner strength and consoling evidence of positive echoes emanating from within a person's light as well as her shadow sides. Each of these statements is a magic spell, stitching together a blanket of negativity that is beyond mere language.

Acknowledge that these affirmations are transformative spells which can help make you change your mind. This habit becomes a ritual of sacred self-love, guiding you through the dance of your light and darkness. By tapping into this source of affirmations, you will see your development as an individual as you not only become more empowered but also magical. Such a transformation not only impacts you but also spreads a positive light that extends and touches those around you, helping them in their own personal development.

1. **"I am in tune with the natural world, and its energy flows through me."**

2. **"I embrace the shadows within me, knowing they hold the keys to my growth."**

3. **"My intuition is my greatest ally, guiding me in all aspects of life."**

4. **"I am a witch, a weaver of spells, and a creator of my own magickal reality."**

5. **"The elements are my allies, and I honor their presence in my craft."**

6. **"I am grounded, balanced, and connected to the Earth's wisdom."**

7. **"My magickal practice is a reflection of my authentic self, and I embrace it fully."**

8. **"I trust the cycles of the moon and the seasons, knowing they bring transformation."**

9. **"I radiate positive energy and attract abundance into my life."**

10. **"I am a witch, and my magick is a force for love, healing, and positive change."**

11. "I am a vessel of light, dispelling negativity and inviting positive energy into my life."

12. "Every step I take is a dance with the universe, creating harmony in my journey."

13. "I am a vessel of light, dispelling negativity and inviting positive energy into my life."

14. "I release what no longer serves me, making room for growth and positive change."

15. "I release negativity and invite abundance into my life."

16. "My intentions are clear, and my magick is strong."

17. "I embrace the power of transformation and welcome positive change into my life."

18. "My words and intentions hold power, shaping the energy around me."

19. "The universe supports my journey, and I am open to receiving its abundant blessings."

20. "I am a powerful witch, manifesting my desires with ease and grace."

Chapter 6

Embrace the Shadows A Guided Meditation

This Guided Meditation holds significant importance in your practice for several reasons:

Establishing a Sacred Space: This meditation helps you create a sacred and safe space within your mind. The meditation's initial step of grounding and protection is crucial for ensuring your emotional and psychological well-being during this process. It instills a sense of safety and stability, allowing you to explore their shadows with confidence.

Connecting with Inner Guidance: The introduction of your inner guide is critical. You may find that you need guidance and support during your shadow work. This luminous figure represents your inner wisdom and strength. In shadow work, it's easy to feel overwhelmed by the darkness within, and having this inner guide provides a comforting presence that offers wisdom, support, and reassurance.

Mirror of Self-Reflection: The practice of using visualization in the mirror of self-reflection invites you to confront your shadow self with compassion rather than judgment. Engaging in shadow work entails the courageous acceptance of your darker characters within your mind—embracing fears, acknowledging insecurities, and tending to unresolved wounds. This guided meditation offers a well-organized and secure avenue to start this cathartic journey.

Guided Meditation:

Meditation creates the necessary mental and emotional environment for a safe exploration of the self. By offering grounding, protection, inner guidance, and a method for confronting your shadow self, this meditation empowers you to inquire about your subconscious with confidence and a sense of preparedness.

Grounding and Protection:
    Create a peaceful space for your meditation, a tranquil area where disruptions are unlikely. Settle into a comfortable position—whether sitting or lying down—close your eyes, and inhale deeply to anchor yourself in the present moment. Envision roots extending from the base of your spine, burrowing deep into the Earth, merging with its stable energy. Picture a golden shield of light enveloping you, acting as a barrier against negativity and distractions. As you start the grounding process, affirm to yourself that you are cocooned in a safe and secure sacred space. Let the burdens of worries and concerns dissipate, allowing a serene calmness to wash over you.

Entering the Sacred Forest:
    In your minds eye, envision yourself standing on the cusp of a mystical forest pulsating with ageless energy and wisdom. You are dressed in your witchy attire, and you carry with you all the

tools and materials you'll need for your shadow work, you stand at the entrance of this esoteric woodland. Immerse yourself in a moment of awe as you take in the forest's breathtaking beauty—listen to the leaves whispering in the wind and relish the cool, invigorating breeze caressing your skin. The fragrance of earth and flourishing foliage envelops your senses, forging a deep connection to the natural world and the unseen energies that surround you.

Meeting Your Inner Guide:

   As you venture deeper into the forest, you encounter a wise and luminous figure. This is your inner guide, a source of support and wisdom on your shadow work journey. The guide emanates a warm, reassuring energy. Approach them and take in their presence, allowing yourself to connect with their energy. Their eyes reflect a deep pool of knowledge and compassion. You may ask them for guidance or protection during your shadow work, knowing that their wisdom is here to assist you throughout your journey.

The Clearing of Self-Reflection:

   Your inner guide leads you to a tranquil clearing in the forest, illuminated by the soft, golden light of the setting sun. In the center of the clearing, you notice a large, ancient mirror reflecting your image. This is the Mirror of Self-Reflection, an artifact that has witnessed the journeys of countless witches before you. Step closer to the mirror, and take a deep breath. The clearing is filled with a sense of peace and serenity, creating the perfect atmosphere for self-exploration.

Facing Your Shadow:

   Now, gaze into the mirror, allowing your shadow self to emerge. This is the part of you that holds your fears, insecurities, and past wounds. Witness your shadow self without judgment. Embrace the emotions that arise, knowing that you are safe and protected in this space. As you look into the mirror, your shadow self takes shape before you. You may see their eyes filled with sorrow or pain, but also the potential for healing and transformation.

Acceptance and Healing:

   Engage in a dialogue with your shadow self. Acknowledge the pain and experiences it represents. Offer words of acceptance, love, and compassion. Feel a profound sense of forgiveness and understanding as you communicate with this aspect of yourself. The clearing seems to resonate with the echoes of your words, enveloping you in a warm, healing energy. Your shadow self, once distant and guarded, begins to soften in response to your compassionate words.

Transformation and Integration:

   As you continue this conversation, see your shadow self begin to transform, becoming less fearful and more luminous. Witness the integration of your shadow into your whole self, feeling a sense of wholeness and empowerment. As your shadow self absorbs the love and understanding you've extended, it undergoes a transformation. Its once dark and heavy form now radiates with a softer, more vibrant light. This transformation signifies the merging of your shadow and conscious self, a powerful and unifying process.

Gratitude and Closure:

Express gratitude to your inner guide and the Mirror of Self-Reflection for their assistance and guidance. The forest and the mirror seem to glow with appreciation as you convey your thanks. This sense of gratitude deepens your connection to the energies of the sacred space.

Returning to Reality:

Slowly bring your awareness back to your physical surroundings. Feel the ground beneath you, and become aware of your breath. Open your eyes, knowing that you are prepared for your shadow work journey, equipped with newfound wisdom and strength. As you return to your physical space, carry with you the warmth, acceptance, and empowerment you've experienced in the sacred forest. You are ready to embark on your shadow work journey, knowing that you can always return to this meditation whenever you need guidance and support on your transformative path of self-discovery.

Chapter 7

Awakening the Shadows: Initiation Ritual

Acknowledgment and Acceptance of the Shadow Self:

Shadow work involves exploring the hidden and suppressed aspects of your psyche, including fears, insecurities, and past traumas. This initiation ritual plays an important role in this process by formally acknowledging the existence of your shadow self. This acknowledgment is a step towards accepting the totality of your being. It encourages you to face your inner darkness without fear. By completing this ritual this will signal your readiness to confront your shadow self head-on.

Dedication to Personal Transformation:

This act of self-dedication signifies the importance of the work ahead. This declaration of intent becomes a cornerstone, a crucial driving force that sustains motivation and resilience throughout the entire shadow work journey, offering the strength needed to persist in the face of challenges and adversities.

As the ritual unfolds, it bestows upon you the power to not only acknowledge but also embrace your inner darkness with acceptance and courage. This empowerment becomes both a catalyst and a sanctuary, guiding you through the intricate labyrinth of serious self-discovery and transformation. It serves as a beacon of strength, propelling you forward while safeguarding the sacred space in which the transformative process of shadow work unfolds.

This simple yet potent ritual is carefully crafted to initiate your shadow work journey, employing the symbolic language of herbs, crystals, and candles. The choice of these elements adds depth to the ritual, connecting you with the ancient wisdom and energies they represent. It is recommended to perform this ritual in a quiet, sacred space, creating an environment conducive to introspection and spiritual exploration.

Materials Needed:

1. A white candle - representing clarity and illumination
2. A black candle - symbolizing the shadow
3. A piece of obsidian or smoky quartz - for grounding and protection
4. A small dish of dried mugwort or wormwood - for dream work and accessing the subconscious
5. A journal and pen.
6. A comfortable and quiet space.

Ritual Steps:

1. Preparation:
   Begin by preparing your sacred space. Cleanse the area with a smoke cleanse with incense, or your preferred method of purification. Light the white candle on the left and the black candle on the right. Place the obsidian or smoky quartz in front of you.

2. Centering and Grounding:
   Sit comfortably, close your eyes, and take several deep breaths. Imagine roots extending from your spine into the Earth, grounding you. As you breathe, feel yourself becoming centered and connected.

3. Invocation:
   Call upon your guides, ancestors, or deities to assist you in your shadow work journey. Ask for their guidance, support, and protection throughout the process.

4. Herbal Preparation:
   Take a small pinch of dried mugwort or wormwood and place it in your dominant hand. Close your eyes, and set your intention for the shadow work you are about to undertake. Ask for clarity, insight, and courage.

5. Candle Visualization:
   Focus your gaze on the white candle's flame. Imagine it illuminating your inner world, dispelling darkness, and revealing your shadow self. Hold this visualization for a few minutes.

6. Candle Affirmation:
   Light the black candle, saying, "I embrace my shadow self with love and acceptance. As this candle burns, so do I release my fears and doubts."

7. Shadow Work Entry:
   Take a moment to reflect on the aspects of your life and self that you wish to explore during your shadow work. Make a mental note, write it in your journal, or record a voice message on your phone.

8. Burning the Herbal Offering:
   Light the pinch of dried mugwort or wormwood with the black candle's flame. As it smolders, pass it through the white candle's flame. As you do, say, "I journey into the depths of my shadow, seeking truth and healing."

9. Dream Work and Meditation:
   Sit quietly for a few moments, allowing the smoldering herbs to fill the space with their scent. Meditate on your shadow work intentions. If you are engaging in dream work, place the smoldering herbs near your pillow.

10. Journaling:

Open your journal and write down any insights, feelings, or visions that come to you during this ritual. These may be guidance from your shadow self or your guides.

11. Closing and Gratitude:

When you are ready, extinguish the candles, starting with the black one. Express gratitude to your guides, deities, and ancestors for their presence. Close the ritual with a statement of appreciation.

12. Integration:

Take the time to integrate the experiences and insights from the ritual into your daily life and future shadow work practice.

Remember to be patient and gentle with yourself throughout your shadow work process, and feel free to revisit this ritual whenever you need support and guidance.

Chapter 8

Crafting an Empowering Shadow Work Oil

Creating a shadow work oil is a powerful way to enhance your spiritual practice. Each ingredient in this recipe is selected for its properties and correspondences to shadow work:

Ingredients:

- **1/4 cup of base oil (such as grapeseed, almond, or jojoba oil):** The base oil, such as grapeseed, almond, or jojoba, serves as the foundation of the shadow work oil. It acts as a carrier for the essential oils and provides a medium for application. The choice of base oil is personal and should resonate with your skin type and preferences, ensuring a balanced connection between the oil and your body.

- **5-7 drops of frankincense essential oil:** Frankincense is often associated with purification, spiritual growth, and connecting with the divine. It's included to help you purify and elevate your shadow work.

- **5-7 drops of myrrh essential oil:** Myrrh is known for its grounding and protective qualities. It's added to anchor your energy, creating a safe and stable space for shadow exploration.

- **3-5 drops of lavender essential oil (You may also add dried lavender if you feel called to.):** Lavender brings a sense of calm and relaxation. It's included to ease any emotional tension that may arise during shadow work, making the process more manageable.

- **3-5 drops of cedarwood essential oil:** Cedarwood is associated with strength and resilience. It helps you confront your shadow self with courage and determination.

- **A small, clean glass bottle or vial with a tight-sealing cap:** This will be used to store your oil.

Instructions:

1. Setting Intentions: Before you begin, take a moment to set your intention for the shadow work oil. Focus on healing, transformation, and embracing your shadow self. Visualize your intention as clearly as possible.

2. Mixing the Oil: In your glass bottle or vial, pour the base oil, filling it about 3/4 full. Add the drops of essential oils one by one, stating your intention as you do. For example, "I add frankincense to purify and elevate my shadow work." Gently swirl the bottle to mix the oils, allowing them to blend together.

3. Charging and Infusing: Place the sealed bottle in a spot where it can receive both sunlight and moonlight for 24 hours. This charging period helps infuse the oil with the energy of the sun and the moon, enhancing its magical properties.

4. Storing Your Oil: After charging, store the shadow work oil in a cool, dark place. Label the bottle with its purpose and creation date.

How to Use the Witch's Shadow Work Oil:

- **Meditation or Visualization:** Begin your meditation, divination, or shadow work sessions by applying a small amount of the oil to your wrists, neck, or third eye chakra. The oil serves as a potent conduit, fostering a heightened state of consciousness and connection to your inner self. The aromatic essence can deepen the meditative experience, allowing for a more profound exploration of your shadows.

- **Bathing Ritual:** Elevate your pre-shadow work preparation by incorporating the oil into a bathing ritual. Add a few drops to your bathwater and immerse yourself. Visualize the oil enveloping you, forming a protective cocoon that prepares you for the deep exploration of your inner self. The combination of the oil's transformative energy and the water's cleansing properties creates a sacred space for profound self-reflection.

- **Crystal Activation:** Before using crystals or stones in your shadow work practice, apply a small amount of the oil to cleanse, charge, and infuse them with transformative energy. This ritual enhances the crystals' ability to resonate with the intentions of your shadow work, creating a synergistic connection between the crystals and the oil's transformative properties.

- **Anointing Sacred Tools:** Prior to utilizing any tools for divination or shadow exploration rituals, anoint them with the oil. This act imbues your tools with the potent energy of the oil, fostering a harmonious connection between the tools and your intention. The anointing ritual ensures that your tools become conduits for the transformative energy required in shadow work practices.

- **Dream Work Enhancer:** Boost your connection to the dream realm by applying a dab of the oil to your temples and pulse points before sleep or engaging in dream work. The aromatic qualities of the oil enhance your receptivity to vivid and insightful dreams, facilitating a deeper exploration of your shadows in the subconscious realm.

– **Candle Magic Amplification:** If you incorporate candle magic into your shadow work, mix a few drops of the oil with the melted wax before solidifying your spell candle. This adds an extra layer of intention and energy to your candle spells, amplifying the effectiveness of your rituals.

Remember that the true magic lies in your intention and the energy you put into the oil as you create and use it. This witch's shadow work oil is a tool to support your journey of self-discovery and transformation.

Chapter 9

Divining the Shadows

Tarot and oracle cards can be powerful tools for witch's shadow work, as they provide insights and guidance into your inner world. Here, I'll explain how to use these cards for shadow work and then provide three different card spreads with interpretations to aid you in this introspective journey.

Getting Started:

1. Choose Your Deck: Select a tarot or oracle deck that resonates with you and feels appropriate for shadow work. **The idea that someone must buy you your first tarot or oracle deck is a myth that often surrounds these mystical tools. In truth, there is no special requirement for how you acquire your deck. What truly matters is the personal connection you feel with the cards. The journey of selecting your first deck is a unique and personal one, and it should be guided by your own intuition and resonance.**

2. Cleansing and Grounding: Before beginning a reading, cleanse your deck with smoke cleansing or use a bell for sound cleansing, and ground yourself to establish a sacred space for your work. Cleansing and grounding your chosen deck before a reading is an essential preparatory step, as it ensures the purity of the energetic connection between you and the cards.

3. Set Your Intentions: Take a moment to set a clear intention for your shadow work. What aspect of yourself or your life do you wish to explore? Frame your questions or intentions accordingly. These intentions guide your questions and the areas of your inner self or life that you aim to explore, making your readings more purposeful and focused.

The following tarot spreads offer structured approaches to your shadow work, allowing you to look into specific shadow aspects and receive guidance on your path to personal growth. These spreads serve as maps for your inner journey, helping you uncover hidden truths, heal past wounds, and integrate your shadow self into a harmonious whole. Each card in these spreads holds a piece of the puzzle, inviting you to interpret their symbolism and connect with your intuition. The knowledge and insights gained from these readings will assist you in your journey towards healing, and transformation.

-Shadow Unveiling Spread

This spread is designed to identify and explore a specific shadow aspect.

Card 1 - The Shadow Self: This card represents the aspect of yourself or your life that you wish to explore. It serves as a mirror to your shadow.

Card 2 - The Root Cause: This card reveals the underlying cause or origin of this shadow aspect. It may point to past experiences, traumas, or beliefs.

Card 3 - The Healing Path: This card offers guidance on how to heal and integrate this shadow aspect. It provides suggestions for personal growth and transformation.

Interpretation: Analyze each card's symbolism, imagery, and your intuitive impressions. Reflect on the messages they convey, and use them as a starting point for your shadow work.

-The Light and Shadow Harmony Spread

This spread helps you explore the interplay between your light and shadow aspects.

Card 1 - Light Aspect: This card represents a positive, well-integrated aspect of yourself or your life.

Card 2 - Shadow Aspect: This card embodies the shadow aspect you wish to address.

Card 3 - Integration: This card offers guidance on how to reconcile and integrate these two aspects, promoting balance and self-awareness.

Interpretation: Examine the cards in pairs, exploring the relationship between the light and shadow aspects. Consider how they interact, influence each other, and what lessons can be learned from this interplay in your journey towards harmony and wholeness.

-The Path to Self-Discovery Spread

This spread provides guidance on your journey toward self-discovery and personal growth.

Card 1 - The Present Self: This card represents your current state of being, including any shadow aspects.

Card 2 - Obstacles and Challenges: This card reveals the challenges or obstacles you may encounter on your path to self-growth.

Card 3 - Guidance and Insights: This card offers guidance, insights, and solutions for overcoming the obstacles and embracing your shadow for personal growth.

Interpretation: Reflect on the information presented in each card. Consider the challenges and opportunities for growth, and how you can work with your shadow to overcome obstacles and transform into a more authentic and empowered version of yourself on your journey of self-discovery.

Chapter 10

Navigating the Dream Realm

Dreamwork is an incredibly powerful too, especiallyl for those practicing witchcraft. It allows you to access hidden aspects of yourself that require exploration, healing, and integration. Dreams act as portals to the subconscious, offering direct pathways to these hidden aspects of the self. By trying dreamwork, you can gain valuable insights and healing experiences that can help to contribute to your personal growth and empowerment.

The subconscious communicates its wisdom and guidance through the dreamworld. Dreams may manifest as symbols, scenarios, or even interactions with shadow figures. These dream experiences offer an opportunity for you to confront and embrace the aspects of yourself that are often buried or rejected in waking life. By exploring dreams through a witch's lens, you can decipher the hidden messages, confront your fears, and integrate these shadow aspects into your conscious awareness.

To support your dreamwork endeavors, I have created three dream journal templates and interpretation guides. The Symbolic Dream Journal assists you in deciphering the symbolism and emotions embedded in your dreams, shedding light on their relevance to your shadow work. The Lucid Dream Journal offers you a structured approach to documenting lucid dream experiences, encouraging you to highlight shadow figures you may have encountered and extract insights to aid your shadow work. The Ancestral Dream Journal guides you in recording dreams involving ancestral figures, providing space to detail interactions, dialogues, and messages, and explore their implications for your ancestral shadow work.

As you interpret your dreams for shadow work, give special attention to the emotions, symbols, and messages inherent in the dream's context. Search for recurring patterns, symbols, or shadow figures that may act as guides for your exploration. While dream interpretation is a deeply personal endeavor, trusting your intuition and inner wisdom remains key, allowing your dreams to unveil the shadow aspects that yearn for healing and integration.

Three Dream Journal Templates and Interpretation Guides:

-Symbolic Dream Journal Template:

- **Date:** [Date of the dream]
- **Symbols:** List significant symbols or images from the dream.
- **Emotions:** Describe the emotions you felt during the dream.
- **Interpretation:** Reflect on the possible meanings of the symbols and emotions. How do they relate to your shadow work?
- **Actions:** Note any actions or decisions you made in the dream and their significance.

  - **Integration:** Consider how the dream's insights can be applied to your waking life and shadow work.

-Lucid Dream Journal Template:

  - **Date:** [Date of the lucid dream]
  - **Dream Description:** Provide a detailed account of the lucid dream experience.
  - **Lucid Moments:** Highlight any moments in the dream where you were aware that you were dreaming.
  - **Confronting Shadows:** If applicable, describe any shadow figures or aspects you confronted in the lucid dream.
  - **Insights:** Record any insights, wisdom, or guidance gained from the dream.
  - **Action Plan:** Based on the dream's revelations, outline specific actions you plan to take in your shadow work.

-Ancestral Dream Journal Template:

  - **Date:** [Date of the ancestral dream]
  - **Dream Setting:** Describe the dream's setting and any notable features.
  - **Ancestral Encounters:** Detail any interactions with ancestors or familial figures in the dream.
  - **Conversations:** If you engage in conversations, record the dialogues.
  - **Messages:** Identify any messages, wisdom, or guidance received from your ancestors.
  - **Reflection:** Reflect on how the dream connects with your ancestral shadow work and its relevance to your current life.

Chapter 11

Candle Magick to Shed Light on Your Shadows

Candle magic is one of the most common and powerful practices among witches that has extraordinary value to witch's shadow work. It entails a range of practices ranging from intention setting, energy direction and connection to spiritual and subconscious realms via candles. Besides the symbolical representation, candles actively take part in shedding light on the healing and assimilating process of shadow self.

1. Setting Intentions: To light a candle for shadow work is to go beyond just generating brightness. It is an initiation method that gives you the ritualistic opportunity to set in words your intention, and thus inaugurate a trip inside yourself. The color of candle is significant as it incorporates colour magic into your procedure. Since each color has its own unique energy and significance, your described ritual is associated with the shadow that you are trying to understand and heal accordingly.

2. Meditation and Focus: Candle magic provides concentration and focus to your practice of shadow work. Relaxing while staring at a fire held in the silent space with perfectly dimmed lights gives rise to meditative state. During this more evolved consciousness, the practitioners delve into subconscious feelings and thoughts pushing down from fear of emotions, trauma that has not been felt or unfulfilled needs. The flickering flame acts as a point of reference, since it can help during navigation through the layers of unconscious to reveal features which are hidden from consciousness.

3. Symbolic Transformation: On a deeper level, candle magic refers to the changes which come about as a result of shadow work. The Candle's flame portrays a light which is the source of knowledge necessary to face repressed aspects inside the soul. As the flame softly flutters and sways, it reflects the complex and ever-changing shadow self. Like the shadow that waxes and wanes with light, candle magic offers you a symbolic semblance of your personal walk towards wholeness.

Color Correspondences in Candle Magic for Witch's Shadow Work:

When it comes to candle magic and shadow work, each candle color is believed to correspond to specific energies and intentions. Here's a breakdown of what each color signifies:

- **Red Candles**:

Associations: Passion, courage, personal power.

Use: Address fears related to self-confidence, assertiveness, and personal boundaries.

- Orange Candles:

Signifies: Creativity, self-expression, joy.
Use: Explore and heal repressed creative energies and emotional wounds linked to self-expression.

- Yellow Candles:

Represents: Mental clarity, communication, self-esteem.
Use: Delve into issues related to self-worth, effective communication, and self-identity.

- Green Candles:

Associated with: Growth, healing, abundance.
Use: Address issues of scarcity, lack, and self-sabotage in shadow work.

- Blue Candles:

Symbolizes: Calm, communication, emotional healing.
Use: Address repressed emotions, promote emotional awareness, and facilitate healing during shadow work.

- Pink Candles:

Symbolizes: Love, compassion, self-acceptance.
Ideal for: Shadow work focused on healing relationships and cultivating self-love.

- Purple Candles:

Signifies: Spiritual insight, psychic awareness, transformation.
Effective in: Accessing the hidden aspects of the subconscious during shadow work.

- Black Candles:

Associated with: Banishment, protection, deep transformation.
Symbolizes: The shadow self and the process of confronting and understanding it.

- White Candles:

Represents: Purity, healing, illumination.
Often used for: Integrating and healing shadow aspects, symbolizing the light that transforms the shadow.

By understanding these color correspondences and their associations, you can choose the most fitting candle color to align with your specific intentions, ensuring that your rituals are in harmony with the energies you seek to invoke.

When starting with candle magic for shadow work, the selection of the right candle color is an important step in aligning with the specific shadow aspect you intend to explore. This choice holds the key to harnessing the symbolic and energetic properties of the candle, amplifying its role as a guide on your path of healing, and personal growth.

But, in the realm of color magic, the quest for a specific colored candle can sometimes be a challenge. Don't worry though, the versatility of white candles shine through in such situations, offering a universal alternative when the exact color eludes you. Their neutrality allows them to seamlessly adapt to a wide spectrum of purposes and energies, establishing them as a reliable choice for various spellwork. In the world of color magic, it's the intention that weaves the threads of power, and white candles stand as adept conduits for channeling that intention, serving as a dependable option in moments of need.

Chapter 12

Stones of Transformation

Stones and crystals that had been revered for thousands of years in the world of magic play a crucial role as tools to help you understand shadow work. These ancient stones are not just dormant materials; instead, they radiate with kinetic energies that follow the spiritual forces directing your transformation. Selecting the appropriate crystals turns into a spiritual practice as each of its vibrations multiplies your energies and helps guide you towards profound enlightenment.

The process of choosing stone can be rather individual and looks more like personal resonance with various crystals; where each person may have their favorite crystal. Besides the personal connection, understanding of the features these crystals consist of is essential. The right stones are like allies, they help to understand and overcome fears, traumas, and memories subconsciously buried. These stones become signposts in the journey of shadow work moving adepts towards consciousness and integration.

Crystals and Stones for Witch's Shadow Work:

-Obsidian:

Why: Commonly known as the "stone of truth," obsidian is prized for its ability to reveal hidden fears and suppressed emotions, providing clarity and insight into one's shadow.
How: It acts as a protective shield, grounding individuals and offering a secure platform for exploring the depths of the shadow.

2. Smoky Quartz:

Why: With grounding properties, smoky quartz effectively dispels negative energies and emotional blockages, making it an excellent aid in confronting past traumas during shadow work.
How: Its promotion of inner strength fosters empowerment, facilitating a more resilient journey into the shadow.

3. Amethyst:

Why: Renowned for spiritual insight and healing, amethyst aids shadow work by promoting self-awareness and emotional balance.
How: It ensures a harmonious and centered path to self-discovery, enhancing the transformative aspects of the journey.

4. Labradorite:

Why: Labradorite is a great choice for accessing hidden truths and illuminating concealed aspects of the psyche during shadow work.
How: Enhancing intuition and psychic abilities, it guides individuals toward a profound understanding of their shadow self.

5. Black Tourmaline:

Why: As a potent protector, black tourmaline creates a fortress against negative energies, establishing a safe space for shadow exploration.
How: This protective shield enables individuals to delve deeper into the shadow with increased assurance.

6. Moonstone:

Why: Moonstone, with its lunar and feminine attributes, elevates emotional understanding, intuition, and introspection during shadow work.
How: It provides essential support, fostering a deeper connection with the emotional aspects of the shadow self.

7. Lepidolite:

Why: Lepidolite's soothing energy is particularly useful for emotional healing, stress relief, and the release of emotional trauma during shadow work.
How: Its compassionate energy facilitates a gentler journey into the depths of the psyche.

8. Hematite:

Why: Hematite aids in grounding and centering, instilling a sense of balance and fearlessness for confident exploration of the shadow self.
How: It enhances resilience, providing a stable foundation for the shadow work journey.

9. Selenite:

Why: Selenite, with its energy-purifying properties, ensures a clear and tranquil energy field, essential for effective shadow work.
How: Providing a calm, purified space, it supports a focused and transformative shadow work experience.

10. Rhodonite:

Why: Renowned for promoting emotional healing and balance, rhodonite encourages forgiveness and compassion during shadow work.

How: It becomes a valuable companion for addressing deep-seated emotional wounds within the shadow self.

11. Apache Tear:

Why: This obsidian variant is gentle yet powerful, often used for grief and emotional release in trauma-related shadow work.
How: Apache Tear aids in understanding and processing sorrow, offering support during the exploration of emotional depths.

12. Chrysocolla:

Why: Chrysocolla, a stone of communication and empowerment, facilitates honest self-expression and helps release emotional baggage.
How: Beneficial for navigating the complexities of shadow work, it supports open communication and emotional release.

13. Pink Opal:

Why: Associated with healing the heart and resolving emotional trauma, pink opal promotes peace and tranquility during shadow work.
How: It becomes a suitable crystal for addressing emotional wounds and fostering emotional well-being in the shadow self.

14. Dalmatian Jasper:

Why: Known for grounding properties, Dalmatian Jasper aids in maintaining composure during emotional challenges in shadow work.
How: Encouraging a positive outlook, it provides support to those dealing with trauma within the shadow.

15. Blue Lace Agate:

Why: Blue Lace Agate is a calming and soothing stone, aiding in communication and expression during shadow work.
How: Supporting the release of repressed emotions, it becomes a helpful crystal for healing-focused shadow work.

16. Ametrine:

Why: Combining the properties of amethyst and citrine, ametrine promotes mental clarity, balance, and spiritual growth during shadow work.
How: Beneficial for understanding and integrating dualities within the self, it enhances the transformative aspects of the shadow work journey.

17. Sugilite:

Why: Sugilite is associated with emotional healing and protection, encouraging self-forgiveness and self-love in shadow work.
How: Its potent energy addresses past traumas, providing support for transformative experiences within the shadow self.

18. Charoite:

Why: Known for transformative energy, charoite helps break old patterns, assisting in facing fears and understanding deeper aspects of the self during shadow work.
How: It becomes a suitable companion for transformative and introspective experiences within the shadow.

19. Red Jasper:

Why: Red Jasper is a grounding stone that promotes strength and stability, beneficial for those working on personal power, resilience, and survival instincts in shadow work.
How: It provides a stable foundation for exploring and addressing aspects related to personal strength within the shadow self.

20. Prehnite:

Why: Prehnite supports emotional healing and enhances inner knowing, aiding in accessing and understanding buried emotions during shadow work.
How: Useful for self-discovery, it becomes a beneficial crystal for those exploring the depths of their emotional landscape within the shadow.

In the world of crystal magic, having the perfect crystal for your intention can be ideal. However, the versatility of clear quartz offers a universal alternative when the crystal you need is not within reach. Known as the "master healer" among crystals, clear quartz possesses the exceptional ability to amplify and enhance the energy of your intentions.

Cleansing and Charging Crystals and Stones for Witch's Shadow Work:

The effectiveness of your crystals hinges on their cleanliness and liveliness. To ensure they are receptive and ready to support your work, it's vital to cleanse and charge them appropriately. Ensuring the vibrational intensity of your crystals is an crucial aspect of caring for your crystals. The more often you work with a crystal, the more energy it accumulates from various sources, both positive and negative. To maintain your crystals highest effectiveness and prevent energetic imbalances, a recommended practice is to clear all your crystals at least once a month. This routine upkeep helps to reset and rejuvenate the stones, allowing them to resonate with clarity and intention.

However, crystals are intuitive entities, and their responsiveness may vary. If you sense that a particular crystal feels heavier than normal or less responsive, it's probably a signal that it could benefit from a cleansing. Trust your instincts and take the time to purify the individual stone. By attuning to your crystals in this way, you establish a rhythmical connection that heightens their energetic properties and ensures a more beneficial experience in your practices.

Some Ways to Cleanse your Crystals:

1. Water: Rinse your crystal under cool, running water to wash away negative energies. **Ensure you understand the sensitivities of each crystal as some are water-soluble and should not be soaked.**

-Here are a few examples of crystals that you should avoid getting wet:

-Selenite: Selenite is a delicate crystal that can easily dissolve when in contact with water. It's best to keep selenite dry to maintain its integrity.

-Halite: Halite, also known as rock salt, is highly soluble in water. Exposing halite to moisture will cause it to disintegrate.

-Pyrite: Pyrite is a metallic mineral that can rust or tarnish when exposed to water. To preserve its lustrous appearance, it's best to keep pyrite dry.

-Lepidolite: Lepidolite contains lithium, which is water-soluble. Immersing lepidolite in water may cause it to break down or lose its vibrant color.

-Calcite: Different varieties of calcite can be sensitive to water. Some calcite specimens may dissolve, become brittle, or lose their shine when exposed to moisture.

-Sulfur: Sulfur crystals can react with water, forming sulfuric acid. This can be harmful and should be avoided.

Always check the specific properties and care instructions for your crystals, as some may be more sensitive than others.

2. Salt: Place your crystal in a bowl of sea salt, Himalayan salt, or rock salt for a few hours or overnight. **(When practicing witchcraft outdoors, be mindful of using salt in rituals. Excessive salt can harm the environment, affecting soil and vegetation, so consider alternative methods or use sparingly to minimize ecological impact.)**

3. Smoke: Pass your crystal through smoke or incense, visualizing the smoke purifying the crystal's energy.

4. Visualization: Hold your crystal and imagine a radiant, white light washing over it, cleansing away any negative energies.

5. Other Crystals: Some crystals, like selenite and clear quartz, have the ability to cleanse other stones. Place your crystal alongside a cleansing crystal for a few hours.

Some Ways to Charge your Crystals:

1. Sunlight: Position your crystal in direct sunlight, particularly during sunrise or sunset, to allow the sun's energy to infuse your crystal with light.

2. Moonlight: Place your crystal under the light of the full moon, new moon, or any moon phase that aligns with your intention.

3. Earth: Bury your crystal in the earth, such as in your garden, for a day or two to ground and recharge it.

4. Sound: Utilize sound vibrations from singing bowls, bells, or a tuning fork to charge your crystal.

5. Visualization: Hold your crystal in your hand, focus on your intent, and imagine a radiant, loving light filling it with the specific energy you desire.

Chapter 13

Ancestral Echoes

1. Take a closer look at your ancestral lineage and identify a pattern or belief that has been passed down through generations. How does it manifest in your life today?

____
____
____
____
____
____
____
____
____
____

2. Contemplate a traumatic event or experience within your ancestral history. How might this trauma still influence your emotions and behaviors?

____
____
____
____
____
____
____
____
____
____

3. Scrutinize the role of gender and power dynamics in your ancestral lineage. How have these dynamics shaped your own beliefs and relationships?

____
____
____
____
____
____

____
____
____
____
____

4. Uncover any ancestral taboos or secrets that have been hidden within your family. What impact have they had on your sense of self and spirituality?

____
____
____
____
____
____
____
____
____

5. Research into the cultural and spiritual practices of your ancestors. Which ones resonate with you, and how might they be integrated into your own path?

____
____
____
____
____
____
____
____
____

6. Connect with an ancestor who you feel a strong connection to. What wisdom or guidance can they offer in healing ancestral wounds?

____
____
____
____
____

____
____
____
____
____

7. Contemplate your family's history of mental health and emotional struggles. How has this impacted your own mental and emotional well-being?

____
____
____
____
____
____
____
____
____
____

8. Remember any ancestral prejudices or biases that have been passed down. How can you work to dismantle these inherited beliefs?

____
____
____
____
____
____
____
____
____
____
____

9. Ask the ways in which your ancestors may have suppressed their spiritual or intuitive gifts. How can you reclaim and nurture these gifts?

____
____
____
____

10. Go over the impact of colonization or migration on your ancestral lineage. How has this history influenced your sense of belonging and identity?

____

____

____

____

____

____

____

____

____

____

____

11. Inquire into any family curses or patterns of bad luck. How can you break free from these patterns and create a more positive future?

____

____

____

____

____

____

____

____

____

____

12. Reflect on your ancestral relationships with nature and the elements. How can you deepen your own connection with the natural world?

____

____

13. Examine the ancestral role of healers or mystics in your family tree. How can you tap into this lineage to enhance your own spiritual journey?

14. Research any ancestral oaths or promises made by your predecessors. Are there any that you need to release or fulfill in your own life?

15. Dig into the stories of resilience and survival within your ancestral history. How can you draw strength from these stories in your own life?

16. Question the ancestral relationship with the divine or deities. How can you honor and connect with the same spiritual forces?

____

____

____

____

____

____

____

17. Consider any instances of betrayal or trust issues within your ancestral lineage. How do these issues manifest in your own relationships, and how can they be healed?

____

____

____

____

____

____

____

____

18. Explore the concept of family karma and its influence on your life. What steps can you take to release and transmute this karma?

____

____

____
____
____
____
____
____
____
____
____

19. Acknowledge any ancestral symbols, signs, or dreams that have appeared in your life. What messages might they hold for your shadow work?

____
____
____
____
____
____
____
____
____

20. Finally, take a deep dive into your own beliefs about life, death, and the afterlife, as influenced by your ancestors. How can you reinterpret or expand upon these beliefs to better serve your spiritual growth and healing?

____
____
____
____
____
____
____
____
____

Chapter 14

Mirrors and Metamorphosis

1. Think about the ways in which media, culture, and society have shaped your perception of beauty and the ideal body. How have these influences affected your self-image as a witch?

____
____
____
____
____
____
____
____
____
____

2. Analyze any childhood experiences or messages related to your body that still impact your self-esteem today. How can you work to heal and release these influences?

____
____
____
____
____
____
____
____
____
____
____

3. Consider your current self-image as a witch. How does it align with your personal and spiritual values? What changes or affirmations can you make to align your self-image with your true
self?

____
____
____
____
____

____

____

____

____

____

4. Scrutinize the ways in which witchcraft and spirituality have influenced your body image. How can you use your magical practice to enhance your self-esteem and self-acceptance?

____

____

____

____

____

____

____

____

5. Look into any body-related rituals, spells, or affirmations that can help you heal and improve your self-image as a witch.

____

____

____

____

____

____

____

____

____

6. Dig into the symbolism of the body in your magical practice. How can you use this symbolism to redefine and empower your self-image?

____

____

____

____

____

7. Think about any negative self-talk or limiting beliefs you hold about your body. How can you use spellwork or affirmations to transform these beliefs into self-love and self-acceptance?

8. Have a look into your past relationships and how they have shaped your body image. How can you release any past wounds and cultivate a more positive self-image?

9. Explore the concept of divine feminine and divine masculine energies within yourself. How can you balance and embrace these energies to improve your self-image as a witch?

10. Test out your magical tools, clothing, and adornments. Do they empower your self-image as a witch? How can you enhance this aspect of your practice?

____

11. Consider how your self-image affects your magical and ritual practices. Are there any rituals or spells that can help you connect with and love your body more deeply?

____

12. Question the concept of body positivity and self-acceptance within the witchcraft community. How can you contribute to a more inclusive and empowering environment for all witches?

____

____

____

____

____

____

____

____

____

13. Think about how you can use herbs and crystals to enhance your self-image and self-esteem as a witch. Which herbs and crystals resonate with your intentions?

____

____

____

____

____

____

____

____

____

14. Feel the connection between your physical body and your intuition. How can you use this connection to boost your self-confidence and self-image as an intuitive witch?

____

____

____

____

____

____

____

____

____

15. Look into the role of dance, movement, and embodiment in your magical practice. How can you use these practices to strengthen your connection with and appreciation for your body?

____

____

16. Explore any deities or archetypes that align with your body image journey. How can you invoke their energy and guidance to empower your self-image?

17. Probe into the impact of self-care and self-love rituals on your self-image as a witch. How can you integrate these practices into your daily life and magical work?

18. Inspect the ways in which your body is a sacred vessel for your magical and spiritual experiences. How can you honor and care for this vessel to enhance your self-image?

19. Consider using mirrors and scrying in witchcraft. How can you use mirrors as tools for self-reflection and self-love in your practice?

20. Finally, think of your unique strengths, talents, and magical abilities as a witch. How can embracing and celebrating these aspects of yourself improve your self-image and self-esteem in your magical journey?

Chapter 15

Weaving the Web of Connection

1. Recall the significant relationships in your life and how they have shaped your spiritual journey. How have past and current relationships influenced your beliefs and practices as a witch?

____

____

____

____

____

____

____

____

____

____

____

2. Explore any recurring patterns or dynamics in your relationships, both romantic and platonic. How do these patterns align with or challenge your values as a witch?

____

____

____

____

____

____

____

____

____

____

____

3. Contemplate the concept of soulmates and spiritual connections in your relationships. How have these connections impacted your personal growth and magical path?

____

____

____

____

4. Think about your ability to set healthy boundaries in your relationships. How can you establish and maintain energetic boundaries in your interactions as a witch?

5. Look into the role of communication in your relationships and the practice of spellwork. How can you use effective communication to enhance your magical partnerships and connections?

6. Brainstorm on any past or current conflicts in your relationships. How can you use witchcraft and spirituality to resolve these conflicts and promote healing?

7. Integrate the influence of the elements and natural cycles into your relationships. How can you align your connections with the energy of the Earth and the elements?

8. Touch upon the idea of love spells and the ethical considerations surrounding them. How can you use love magic responsibly and ethically in your relationships?

9. Interpret on the role of jealousy, envy, and comparison in your relationships. How can you work on releasing these negative emotions and promoting healthier connections?

10. Meditate on the archetype of the witch in mythology and its impact on your relationships. How can you embrace the wisdom and power of the witch archetype in your interactions?

11. Explore your romantic partnerships and their connection to your own self-love and self-worth. How can you use your magical practice to strengthen your self-esteem in relationships?

12. Look into your friendships and the qualities you seek in your chosen spiritual community. How can you foster a sense of belonging and support in these relationships?

13. Consider the concept of energetic cords and attachments in relationships. How can you cleanse and release any unhealthy attachments to promote healing and growth?

14. Check out the role of divination and tarot in understanding your relationship dynamics. How can you use these tools to gain insight into your connections with others?

15. Remember the influence of your ancestors' relationship patterns on your own. How can you heal and transform ancestral patterns to create healthier relationships in your life?

16. Consider the ways in which your relationships affect your sense of magic and personal power. How can you encourage and support each other's spiritual journeys within your relationships?

17. Analyze the concept of reciprocity and balance in your relationships. How can you ensure that energy and effort are equally exchanged for mutual benefit?

18. Dive into the impact of trauma and past wounds on your relationships. How can you use shadow work and healing practices to address these issues and create healthier dynamics?

19. Question the role of forgiveness and compassion in your relationships. How can you use your magical practice to cultivate forgiveness and promote healing in your connections?

20. Finally, research the idea of sacred unions and partnerships in witchcraft. How can you honor and celebrate the sacredness of your most meaningful relationships within your magical path?

Chapter 16

Sensual Liberation

1. Recall your earliest memories or influences related to sexuality and sensuality. How have these early experiences shaped your beliefs and behaviors as a witch?

____

____

____

____

____

____

____

____

____

____

2. Explore your connection between sexuality and your spiritual path. How does your sensuality empower or hinder your magical practice?

____

____

____

____

____

____

____

____

____

____

____

3. Take a closer look at any past traumas or negative experiences related to sexuality. How can you work on healing and releasing these wounds through witchcraft and self-empowerment?

____

____

____

____

____

____

4. Uncover the influence of societal norms and expectations on your views of sexuality and sensuality. How can you challenge and redefine these influences to embrace your authentic self?

____

____

____

____

____

____

____

____

____

____

5. Research the symbolism of sexuality and sensuality in your magical practice. How can you use these energies to amplify your spells, rituals, and intentions?

____

____

____

____

____

____

____

____

____

____

6. Feel through any guilt or shame you may hold regarding your own desires and pleasures. How can you work on releasing these inhibitions and embracing your sensuality as a source of strength?

____

____

____

____

7. Recall the connection between your sensuality and your relationship with your body. How can you improve your body image and self-love through your magical practices?

____

____

____

____

____

____

____

____

____

____

8. Look into the role of sacred sexuality and tantric practices in your spiritual journey. How can you use these practices to connect with your inner divine and cultivate greater pleasure and intimacy in your life?

____

____

____

____

____

____

____

____

____

____

9. Go over any repressive religious or cultural backgrounds that may have impacted your views on sexuality. How can you free yourself from these limitations and embrace your authentic desires?

____

10. Consider the use of aphrodisiac herbs and oils in your magical rituals. How can you incorporate these natural allies to enhance your sensuality and pleasure?

11. Explore your sexual energy as a source of power and manifestation in your magical practice. How can you channel this energy to create your desired reality?

12. Inquire about your relationship with your own desires and fantasies. How can you express and honor these aspects of yourself without judgment or inhibition?

____
____
____
____
____
____
____
____
____
____

13. Look into the power of sexual symbolism in your witchcraft. How can you use this symbolism to amplify your magical intentions and desires?

____
____
____
____
____
____
____
____
____
____
____

14. Do you enjoy working with the influence of lunar phases and natural cycles for your sensuality and sexual energy. How can you align with these energies to enhance your pleasure and connection with your inner self?

____
____
____
____
____
____
____
____
____
____

15. Uncover the concept of consent and boundaries in your sexual and magical interactions. How can you ensure that your experiences are safe, respectful, and consensual?

____

____

____

____

____

____

____

____

____

____

16. Feel the connection between sensuality and the five senses in your magical practice. How can you use sensory experiences to deepen your connection with pleasure and empowerment?

____

____

____

____

____

____

____

____

____

____

____

17. Research the concept of body rituals and self-care as a means of enhancing your sensuality. How can you pamper and celebrate your body as a sacred vessel of pleasure and magic?

____

____

____

____

____

____

____

____

____

____

18. Reckon with your relationships and partnerships, and how they affect your sensuality and sexuality. How can you maintain healthy boundaries and open communication in these connections?

____

____

____

____

____

____

____

____

____

____

19. Remember the power of affirmations and mantras in cultivating a positive and empowered view of your own sensuality. How can you use words and intentions to transform your beliefs and   behaviors?

____

____

____

____

____

____

____

____

____

____

20. Finally, see about the idea of self-love, self-acceptance, and self-pleasure as essential components of shadow work related to sexuality and sensuality. How can you practice self-compassion   and   empowerment   in   this   realm   of   your   life?

____

____

____

____

____

____

____

Chapter 17

Facing the Shadows Within

1. Question your deepest fears and anxieties related to your witchcraft and spiritual practices. What is the source of these fears, and how have they held you back?
____
____
____
____
____
____
____
____
____
____
____

2. Look into the connection between fear and your magical abilities. How have your fears affected your intuition, spellwork, or rituals?
____
____
____
____
____
____
____
____
____
____
____

3. Acknowledge the influence of societal stigma on your fears about being a witch. How can you challenge and release these external pressures to authentically embrace your path?
____
____
____
____
____
____
____

4. Take a deep dive into the concept of protection and warding in witchcraft. How can you use these practices to alleviate fear and anxiety in your magical work?

5. Analyze the role of past traumas in triggering fear and anxiety in your spiritual journey. How can you work on healing and releasing these emotional wounds?

6. Look into the impact of fear on your connection to the divine or higher powers. How can you cultivate trust and surrender in your spiritual practice to reduce anxiety?

____

____

____

____

____

7. Have a look into the symbolism of darkness and the shadow in your witchcraft. How can you use shadow work to confront and transform your fears?

____

____

____

____

____

____

____

____

____

____

8. Recall your fear of judgment and criticism from others regarding your spiritual path. How can you find confidence and resilience in the face of external opinions?

____

____

____

____

____

____

____

____

____

9. Question the concept of fear as a guardian of hidden knowledge. How can you approach your fears with curiosity and a willingness to learn from them?

____

____

____

____

____
____
____
____
____
____

10. Feel out the influence of fear and anxiety in your spellcasting. How can you develop a strong sense of empowerment and confidence in your magical abilities?

____
____
____
____
____
____
____
____
____
____

11. Think about your fear of failure or making mistakes in your witchcraft. How can you reframe these fears as valuable learning experiences?

____
____
____
____
____
____
____
____
____

12. Remember the role of community and support in confronting your fears as a witch. How can you connect with like-minded individuals who understand and encourage your path?

____
____
____
____

____

____

____

____

____

____

____

13. Feel the fear of persecution and discrimination that may be rooted in your ancestral history. How can you honor and transcend this ancestral fear in your practice?

____

____

____

____

____

____

____

____

____

____

14. Look into the concept of grounding and centering as tools to alleviate fear and anxiety. How can you incorporate these practices into your daily life?

____

____

____

____

____

____

____

____

____

15. Inspect the influence of lunar phases and the cycles of nature in managing your emotional states and reducing anxiety. How can you align with these natural rhythms to find balance and calm?

____

____

16. Lament on the connection between fear and manifestation. How can you use your thoughts and intentions to manifest a reality free from unnecessary anxieties?

17. Research the role of herbs, crystals, and other magical tools in alleviating fear and anxiety. How can you incorporate these allies into your practice for emotional support?

18. Feel the power of affirmations and mantras in addressing fear and anxiety. How can you use positive words and intentions to reprogram your thoughts and beliefs?

19. Think into the idea of surrender and letting go in your magical practice. How can you release the need for control and, in turn, reduce fear and anxiety?

20. Finally, meditate on the concept of self-compassion and self-care as essential components of shadow work. How can you be gentle with yourself as you confront and transform your fears and anxieties, knowing that you are on a path of growth and healing?

Chapter 18

Your Beliefs Unveiled

1. Take a closer look at the core beliefs of your spiritual path. How have these beliefs evolved and transformed over time, and do they still resonate with your true self?

____
____
____
____
____
____
____
____
____
____

2. Uncover any doubts or uncertainties you may have about your spiritual path. What is the source of these doubts, and how can you work on resolving them?

____
____
____
____
____
____
____
____
____
____
____

3. Connect with the influence of external authorities and dogmas on your spiritual beliefs. How can you challenge and reshape these influences to create a more authentic belief system?

____
____
____
____
____
____

4. Go over the concept of faith in your magical and spiritual journey. How can you cultivate a deeper sense of trust and belief in your own power and intuition?

____

____

____

____

____

____

____

____

____

____

____

5. Dig into the role of shadow work and inner exploration in confronting and transforming spiritual doubts. How can you use shadow work to uncover and address these doubts?

____

____

____

____

____

____

____

____

____

____

6. Acknowledge the symbolism of sacred texts and spiritual literature in your beliefs. How can you reinterpret and adapt these texts to better align with your evolving spirituality?

____

____

____

____

____

7. Explore the concept of divine beings or deities in your spiritual practice. How can you challenge and redefine your understanding of these entities to better fit your beliefs and experiences?

____
____
____
____
____
____
____
____
____
____
____

8. Look more into the influence of cultural or ancestral beliefs on your spirituality. How can you honor and integrate these influences while staying true to your own path?

____
____
____
____
____
____
____
____
____
____
____

9. Take a deep dive into the impact of fear, guilt, or shame related to your spiritual beliefs. How can you release these negative emotions and align with a more empowering belief system?

____
____
____
____

10. Think about the concept of synchronicity and signs in your spiritual journey. How can you use these experiences to reaffirm your beliefs and build a stronger sense of faith?

11. Analyze the role of intuition and personal revelation in shaping your spiritual beliefs. How can you trust your inner guidance and use it to deepen your faith?

12. Take into account the use of divination tools in challenging and reevaluating your spiritual beliefs. How can tarot, runes, or other divination methods help you gain clarity and insight into your path?

13. Look into the connection between your spiritual beliefs and your daily rituals and practices. How can you ensure that your actions align with your true beliefs and values?

14. Determine any influence of sacred symbols and rituals in your spiritual path. How can you use these tools to strengthen your connection to your belief system?

15. Find the role of community and like-minded individuals in reinforcing or challenging your spiritual beliefs. How can you engage in healthy dialogue and discussions to expand your perspective?

16. Dig into your past experiences and spiritual awakenings. How have these experiences shaped your beliefs, and how can you continue to grow and evolve in your spirituality?

17. Question the concept of universal truths and cosmic laws in your spiritual beliefs. How can you align with these principles while also embracing the uniqueness of your path?

18. Analyze the power of meditation and mindfulness in challenging and transforming your spiritual beliefs. How can these practices help you connect with your inner wisdom and truth?

____

____

____

____

____

____

____

____

____

____

19. Think about your connection with the natural world and its impact on your spirituality. How can you use nature as a source of inspiration and affirmation for your beliefs?

____

____

____

____

____

____

____

____

____

____

20. Finally, feel the concept of faith in yourself as the ultimate source of your power and magic. How can you build unwavering belief in your own abilities and potential within your spiritual journey?

____

____

____

____

____

____

____

____

____

____

Chapter 19

Clarifying Your Journey

1. Think about your career and how it aligns with your life purpose as a witch. Are there aspects of your current job that empower or hinder your spiritual journey?

____

____

____

____

____

____

____

____

____

____

2. Take into consideration any fears or doubts you may have about pursuing a career in witchcraft or spirituality. How can you work on transforming these fears into opportunities for growth?

____

____

____

____

____

____

____

____

____

____

3. Review the influence of societal expectations and norms on your career choices. How can you challenge these influences to follow your true calling as a witch?

____

____

____

____

____

____
____
____
____
____

4. Inspect the role of financial stability in your career decisions. How can you create a career that aligns with your spiritual path while ensuring financial security?

____
____
____
____
____
____
____
____
____
____
____

5. Consider the concept of manifestation and intention setting in your career and life purpose. How can you use your magical skills to manifest the career and life you desire?

____
____
____
____
____
____
____
____
____
____
____
____

6. Remember the impact of past failures or setbacks on your career confidence. How can you use your magical practice to overcome these challenges and build resilience?

____
____
____
____
____

7. Think about the role of passion and purpose in your career choices. How can you infuse your work with a sense of meaning and fulfillment that aligns with your spiritual journey?

8. Review the influence of any mentors and guides who shape your career path. How can you find or connect with mentors who support and inspire your spiritual aspirations?

9. Consider the concept of shadow work in addressing and overcoming career-related fears and self-sabotage. How can you use shadow work to heal and empower your career choices?

10. Look into the symbolism of the elements and their connection to your life purpose. How can you align your career with the elemental energies that resonate with your path?

11. Brainstorm on the role of divination and oracle cards in gaining insights about your career and life purpose. How can you use these tools to clarify your path and make informed decisions?

12. Integrate the power of intention setting and ritual in creating a fulfilling career. How can you use ritual practices to set clear intentions for your life purpose and career success?

____
____
____
____
____
____
____
____
____

13. Give thought to your unique skills and talents as a witch. How can you leverage your magical abilities to enhance your career and make a positive impact in the world?

____
____
____
____
____
____
____
____
____

14. Explore the concept of self-worth and how it relates to your career choices. How can you work on strengthening your self-esteem and self-belief in the pursuit of your life purpose?

____
____
____
____
____
____
____
____

15. Touch upon the role of meditation and mindfulness in clarifying your career and life purpose. How can these practices help you connect with your inner wisdom and guidance?

____

16. Interpret the influence of your spiritual values and ethics in making career decisions. How can you ensure that your work aligns with your spiritual principles and beliefs?

17. Ponder the connection between your career and your relationships. How can you maintain healthy boundaries and supportive connections while pursuing your life purpose?

18. Examine the influence of self-doubt and imposter syndrome in your career choices. How can you use self-empowerment and positive affirmations to overcome these challenges?

19. Look into the symbolism of symbols, signs, and synchronicities in your career path. How can you use these messages from the universe to guide your choices and actions?

20. Finally, incorporate the concept of living authentically and unapologetically in alignment with your life purpose as a witch. How can you embrace and embody your true calling with confidence and joy?

Chapter 20

Tending the Earth Within

1. Review your personal connection with the natural world and its influence on your magical and spiritual beliefs. How can you deepen your bond with nature to promote a more sustainable and ecologically-conscious lifestyle?

____

____

____

____

____

____

____

____

____

____

2. Weigh any feelings of disconnection or apathy toward environmental issues. How can you use your magical practice to reignite your passion for ecological causes?

____

____

____

____

____

____

____

____

____

____

3. Deliberate on your daily habits and lifestyle choices and their impact on the environment. How can you make conscious and sustainable choices in your everyday life as a witch?

____

____

____

____

____

____

4. Call to mind the role of consumerism and materialism in your life. How can you embrace a simpler, more eco-friendly lifestyle in alignment with your magical path?

____
____
____
____
____
____
____
____
____
____

5. Look into the symbolism of the elements and their connection to ecological principles. How can you honor and protect the elements in your magical work to promote environmental healing?

____
____
____
____
____
____
____
____
____

6. Be curious about the influence of ancestral practices and traditions on your ecological beliefs. How can you honor and integrate these ancestral influences to support eco-conscious living?

____
____
____

____

____

____

____

____

____

____

7. Speculate on the impact of eco-anxiety and environmental concerns on your emotional well-being. How can you use your magical practice to find peace and empowerment in the face of ecological challenges?

____

____

____

____

____

____

____

____

____

____

8. Evaluate the concept of sacred spaces and rituals in your connection with nature. How can you create and maintain sacred spaces that honor and protect the environment?

____

____

____

____

____

____

____

____

____

____

9. Meditate on your relationship with plants, animals, and the natural world. How can you work on connecting with and preserving the biodiversity of the Earth through your magical practices?

____

____

____

____

____

____

____

____

____

____

10. Give some thought to the role of eco-activism and advocacy in your life. How can you use your magical abilities and spiritual voice to raise awareness and contribute to positive environmental change?

____

____

____

____

____

____

____

____

____

____

11. Remember the power of herbalism and plant magic in ecological healing. How can you use these practices to support the well-being of the Earth and its ecosystems?

____

____

____

____

____

____

____

____

____

____

12. Look into the concept of recycling, repurposing, and sustainable crafting in your magical and creative endeavors. How can you reduce waste and promote eco-conscious crafting?

13. Analyze the connection between energy conservation and your magical practice. How can you use energy-efficient practices and alternative energy sources to reduce your ecological footprint?

14. Take into account the role of water, land, and air purification in your magical rituals. How can you use these practices to cleanse and protect the environment in addition to your personal space?

15. Discuss the impact of pollution and waste on the natural world. How can you use your magical practice to cleanse and purify the environment and promote healing?

____
____
____
____
____
____
____
____
____
____

16. Assess the concept of ritual gardening and permaculture as a means of connecting with and nurturing the Earth. How can you create a sustainable and abundant garden that supports local ecosystems?

____
____
____
____
____
____
____
____
____
____

17. Investigate the role of meditation and mindfulness in fostering a deep sense of connection with nature. How can these practices help you appreciate and protect the environment more effectively?

____
____
____
____
____
____
____
____

18. Observe your role as a steward of the Earth and its resources. How can you use your magical abilities to honor and protect the environment as a responsible custodian?

____
____
____
____
____
____
____
____
____
____

19. Think about the concept of eco-shamanism and journeying to connect with the spirits of the land. How can you work with these spirits to receive guidance and support for your ecological efforts?

____
____
____
____
____
____
____
____
____
____
____

20. Finally, consider the principle of collective consciousness and global unity in ecological healing. How can you use your magical practice to contribute to the collective energy of positive change and environmental protection on a larger scale?

____
____
____
____
____
____

Chapter 21

Wealth's Harvest

1. Meditate on your earliest memories and experiences related to money. How have these early impressions shaped your current beliefs about wealth and abundance?

____
____
____
____
____
____
____
____
____
____

2. Look into your relationship with material possessions and consumerism. How do these beliefs impact your sense of financial abundance and well-being as a witch?

____
____
____
____
____
____
____
____
____
____

3. Review any fears or anxieties you have about scarcity and financial insecurity. How can you work on transforming these fears into a mindset of abundance and prosperity?

____
____
____
____
____
____

4. Take into account your self-worth and its connection to your financial situation. How can you enhance your self-esteem to attract greater financial prosperity?

____

____

____

____

____

____

____

____

____

____

5. Journey into the influence of societal expectations and norms on your financial beliefs. How can you challenge these influences to embrace your unique path to abundance?

____

____

____

____

____

____

____

____

____

6. Imagine the power of intention setting and manifestation in attracting wealth. How can you use your magical practice to set clear financial goals and manifest abundance?

____

____

____

____

____

7. Give thought to the concept of money as energy. How can you improve the flow of financial energy in your life to experience greater prosperity?

____

____

____

____

____

____

____

____

____

8. Dig into your beliefs about deserving wealth and prosperity. How can you release any guilt or unworthiness related to financial abundance?

____

____

____

____

____

____

____

____

____

9. Check out the role of gratitude and abundance rituals in your magical practice. How can you use these rituals to shift your focus toward the abundance already present in your life?

____

____

____

10. Analyze the symbolism of coins, currency, and wealth in your magical work. How can you use these symbols to amplify your financial intentions and rituals?

____

____

____

____

____

____

____

____

____

____

11. Determine the impact of generosity and charitable giving on your financial abundance. How can you use acts of kindness to invite greater prosperity into your life?

____

____

____

____

____

____

____

____

____

____

12. Study the role of networking and connecting with like-minded individuals in your financial journey. How can you build supportive relationships that empower your financial success?

____

____

____

13. Think about your current financial goals and aspirations. How can you set specific, achievable goals aligned with your path as a witch?

14. Discuss the idea of the concept of passive income and multiple streams of revenue. How can you diversify your income sources to create financial stability?

15. Explore the influence of your ancestors' financial beliefs and practices. How can you honor and learn from their experiences to shape your own path to prosperity?

16. Think on the role of patience and perseverance in achieving long-term financial goals. How can you stay committed to your path to abundance, even in the face of challenges?

17. Search into the idea of ethical money management and conscious spending. How can you align your financial decisions with your spiritual and ethical values?

18. Take into account the use of crystal and herbal magic in attracting financial prosperity. How can you incorporate these magical allies into your wealth and abundance rituals?

19. Give thought to the concept of abundance affirmations and positive money mindset. How can you reframe your beliefs about money to attract greater wealth and success?

20. Finally, inquire into the idea of giving back and sharing your financial abundance with others. How can you use your prosperity to contribute positively to your community and the world as a whole?

Chapter 22

Whispers of the Four Elements

Earth (Stability and Grounding):

1. How do you feel connected to the element of Earth in your life? Are there moments when you've felt grounded or stable?

____

____

____

____

____

____

____

____

____

2. Inspect any fears or insecurities related to material possessions, stability, or your physical body. How might these relate to your Earth element shadow?

____

____

____

____

____

____

____

____

____

3. Analyze your relationship with nature and the outdoors. How does it impact your sense of grounding and stability?

____

____

____

____

____

____

____

____

____

____

4. Look into the practical aspects of your life, such as finances and home. How might your shadow self affect your approach to these areas?

____

____

____

____

____

____

____

____

____

____

Air (Intellect and Communication):

5. How do you experience the element of Air in your thought processes and communication? Are there moments of clarity or confusion?

____

____

____

____

____

____

____

____

____

____

6. Inquire into any communication challenges, fears of speaking your truth, or intellectual insecurities you may have.

____
____
____
____
____
____
____
____
____
____

7. Think about how your thought patterns and beliefs influence your shadow self. Are there mental patterns you'd like to explore or transform?

____
____
____
____
____
____
____
____
____
____

8. Examine your relationship with technology and information. How might these areas be linked to your Air element shadow?

____
____
____
____
____
____
____
____
____

Fire (Passion and Willpower):

9. How do you express the element of Fire in your life, especially in terms of passion, desires, and willpower?

____
____
____
____
____
____
____
____
____
____

10. Check on any suppressed passions or desires and how they may relate to your shadow self.

____
____
____
____
____
____
____
____
____
____
____

11. Meditate on your temper, anger, or impulsiveness. How have these emotions affected your life, and how can you harness their positive aspects?

____
____
____
____
____
____
____
____
____
____

12. Look into the role of motivation, ambition, and taking action in your life. How does your shadow self influence your drive?

____
____
____
____
____
____
____
____
____
____
____

Water (Emotions and Intuition):

13. How do you experience the element of Water in your emotional life and intuitive abilities? Are you in touch with your feelings and instincts?

____
____
____
____
____
____
____
____
____
____

14. Look back on past emotional wounds, fears, or insecurities, and how they might be connected to your Water element shadow.

____
____
____
____
____
____
____
____

15. Think about your dreams, intuition, and psychic abilities. How does your shadow self impact these aspects of your inner world?

____

____

____

____

____

____

____

____

____

____

16. Audit your relationships and connections with others. How do your emotions and intuitive senses influence your interactions?

____

____

____

____

____

____

____

____

____

____

Elemental Balance (Integration):

17. Inquire how a balance of the elements can promote inner harmony and personal growth. How can you incorporate the qualities of Earth, Air, Fire, and Water into your shadow work journey?

____

____

____

____
____
____
____
____
____
____
____

18. Investigate your primary elemental influences. Do you find one element dominating your life, or are they in balance? What lessons might each element hold for you?

____
____
____
____
____
____
____
____
____
____
____

19. Question any rituals or practices that involve working with the elements. How have they influenced your understanding of your shadow self?

____
____
____
____
____
____
____
____
____

20. Imagine an ideal state of elemental balance within yourself. What steps can you take to achieve this balance and address your shadow self through elemental integration?

____
____
____

Chapter 23

Wholeness Within

1. Take into consideration your personal history of physical and mental health. How have these experiences influenced your well-being and spiritual journey as a witch?

____
____
____
____
____
____
____
____
____
____

2. Be curious about any fears or anxieties related to illness and health. How can you work on transforming these fears into a source of empowerment and healing?

____
____
____
____
____
____
____
____
____
____

3. Consider the influence of societal expectations and beauty standards on your self-image and health habits. How can you challenge these influences and cultivate self-love and acceptance?

____
____
____
____
____
____

4. Recall your connection between holistic healing practices and witchcraft. How can your magical and spiritual beliefs support your overall well-being?

5. Take a closer look at the role of self-care and self-compassion in your health and well-being. How can you prioritize self-care rituals that align with your spiritual path?

6. Uncover the impact of ancestral health patterns and traditions on your own well-being. How can you draw wisdom and inspiration from your ancestral lineage to support your health?

7. Feel through your relationship with nature and the elements in relation to your health. How can you harness the healing energies of the natural world to promote well-being?

8. Look into the concept of energetic healing and the use of energy work in addressing physical and emotional health concerns. How can you incorporate energy healing into your self-care routine?

9. Go over the role of balance and moderation in your lifestyle choices. How can you find harmony in your daily routines to support your physical and mental health?

10. Inquire about the symbolism of herbs, crystals, and elements in your healing practices. How can you use these allies to enhance your self-care rituals and well-being?

11. Look into the concept of shadow work in addressing underlying emotional issues that may affect your health. How can you use shadow work to unearth and heal these emotional wounds?

12. Test the use of divination and tarot as tools for gaining insights into your health and well-being. How can you use these practices to guide your self-care decisions?

13. Observe the influence of nutrition and food choices on your health. How can you use your magical practice to cultivate a healthier relationship with food and nourishment?

14. Feel through the concept of movement and physical activity as a means of promoting well-being. How can you incorporate mindful movement practices into your daily life as a witch?

15. Examine the impact of sound healing and music on your emotional and physical well-being. How can you use sound and music to support your holistic health?

16. Review the role of mindfulness and meditation in fostering mental and emotional well-being. How can you use these practices to cultivate a deeper connection with your inner self and reduce stress?

____
____
____
____
____
____
____
____
____
____

17. Explore the idea of incorporating herbal remedies and natural healing as part of your self-care routine. How can you use herbal magic to address specific health concerns and promote healing?

____
____
____
____
____
____
____
____
____

18. Look into the use of affirmation and intention-setting in supporting your mental and emotional health. How can you reframe your thoughts and beliefs to enhance your well-being?

____
____
____
____
____
____
____
____
____
____

19. Weigh in on your relationships and the impact they have on your overall health. How can you establish healthy boundaries and seek supportive connections to improve your well-being?

____
____
____
____
____
____
____
____
____
____

20. Finally, investigate into the concept of holistic healing and the interconnectedness of body, mind, and spirit. How can you work on achieving a state of balance and well-being that supports your spiritual journey as a witch?

____
____
____
____
____
____
____
____
____

Chapter 24

Unraveling the Ties That Bind

1. Recall your earliest memories of family dynamics. How have these early experiences shaped your beliefs and roles within your family?

____

____

____

____

____

____

____

____

____

____

2. Acknowledge any emotional wounds or unresolved conflicts within your family. How can you use your magical and spiritual practices to begin the process of healing and reconciliation?

____

____

____

____

____

____

____

____

____

____

3. Consider the influence of ancestral family patterns and traditions on your own family dynamics. How can you honor and integrate these influences while fostering healthier relationships?

____

____

____

____

____

____

4. Take into consideration your roles and responsibilities within your family. How do these roles align with your true self and your spiritual path, and how can you establish more healthy boundaries?

5. Take a deep dive into the concept of forgiveness and letting go in the context of family dynamics. How can you use your magical practice to release grudges and find emotional freedom?

6. Analyze the impact of communication and open dialogue within your family. How can you use effective communication and magical rituals to foster understanding and connection?

7. Research the symbolism of family in your magical and spiritual beliefs. How can your spiritual path empower and heal family relationships?

____
____
____
____
____
____
____
____
____
____

8. Meditate on the idea of ancestral altars and ancestor veneration as tools for family healing. How can you create an ancestral altar to honor and connect with your family lineage?

____
____
____
____
____
____
____
____
____
____

9. Feel out the role of empathy and compassion in addressing family dynamics. How can you work on cultivating greater empathy and understanding within your family relationships?

____
____

10. Recall your experiences with power dynamics and hierarchies within your family. How can you use your magical abilities to create a more balanced and harmonious family environment?

11. Question the concept of family rituals and traditions. How can you infuse these traditions with intention and magic to enhance your connections and healing within your family?

12. Take into consideration the use of divination and tarot or oracle cards as tools for gaining insights into family dynamics. How can you use divination to gain a deeper understanding of your family relationships?

13. Think about the influence of emotions and energy in family interactions. How can you use energy work and emotional healing to create a more harmonious family environment?

14. Explore the role of personal boundaries and self-care in managing family relationships. How can you prioritize self-care and set clear boundaries within your family interactions?

15. Contemplate the use of symbolic rituals and ceremonies to mark transitions and milestones within your family. How can you create meaningful rituals to strengthen family bonds?

____
____
____
____
____
____
____
____
____
____

16. Meditate on your ancestral traditions and their impact on your family's cultural identity. How can you celebrate and integrate these traditions within your family while still honoring your unique spiritual path?

____
____
____
____
____
____
____
____
____
____

17. Integrate the concept of shadow work within the context of family dynamics. How can you use shadow work to uncover and heal deeper wounds and patterns within your family?

____
____
____
____
____
____
____
____
____

18. Investigate the impact of support and community in addressing family challenges. How can you find or create a support network of like-minded individuals who understand and encourage your family healing efforts?

____

____

____

____

____

____

____

____

____

____

19. Look into your role as a peacemaker and mediator within your family. How can you use your skills to foster harmony and resolution in family conflicts?

____

____

____

____

____

____

____

____

____

____

____

20. Finally, explore the idea of creating a family of choice within your magical and spiritual community. How can you establish and nurture chosen family connections that align with your path and provide a source of love and support?

____

____

____

____

____

____

____

____

Chapter 25

Embrace and Transform

1. Meditate on your earliest memories of rejection or acceptance in your life. How have these early experiences shaped your beliefs about self-acceptance and self-love as a witch?

____
____
____
____
____
____
____
____
____
____

2. Take a closer look at the influence of societal beauty standards and expectations on your self-image and need for external validation. How can you challenge these influences to cultivate a   deeper   sense   of   self-acceptance?

____
____
____
____
____
____
____
____
____
____
____

3. Go over any fears or anxieties you have related to being rejected for your spiritual path or magical practices. How can you work on transforming these fears into sources of self-empowerment?

____
____
____
____
____

4. Uncover the connection between self-acceptance and self-love with your magical and spiritual beliefs. How can your spiritual path support a positive self-image and self-acceptance?

5. Research the role of affirmations and positive intentions in boosting self-acceptance. How can you use these tools to reframe your beliefs and cultivate self-love?

6. Connect with the impact of past rejections and emotional wounds on your self-esteem and self-worth. How can you use your magical practice to heal and release these wounds?

7. Dig into the symbolism of mirrors and reflections in your magical work. How can you use these symbols to promote self-reflection and self-acceptance?

8. Acknowledge the concept of self-compassion and self-care as essential components of self-acceptance and self-love. How can you prioritize self-compassion in your daily life as a witch?

9. Look into the influence of shadow work in addressing deep-seated self-rejection and self-doubt. How can you use shadow work to confront and transform these limiting beliefs?

10. Take into consideration the role of vulnerability and authenticity in self-acceptance. How can you embrace your true self and be open about your spiritual path without fear of rejection?

11. Take a deep dive into the concept of self-empowerment through self-expression. How can you use your creativity and magic to express your authentic self and boost self-acceptance?

12. Think about the use of protection spells and rituals in safeguarding your self-esteem and self-acceptance. How can you create a shield of confidence to ward off external judgment?

13. Analyze the power of meditation and mindfulness in fostering self-acceptance and self-love. How can you use these practices to connect with your inner worth and beauty?

14. Take into account the concept of self-image and its connection to self-acceptance. How can you work on improving your body image and self-love through your magical practices?

15. Look into the role of self-acceptance in embracing your unique path as a witch. How can you find confidence and empowerment in your spiritual journey, regardless of external judgment?

____

____

____

____

____

____

____

____

____

____

16. Find your relationship with self-expression and creativity as tools for promoting self-acceptance. How can you use your creative talents to celebrate your uniqueness and boost self-love?

____

____

____

____

____

____

____

____

____

____

17. Question the idea of self-validation and internal approval as a source of strength. How can you shift your focus from external validation to recognizing your worth from within?

____

____

____

____

____

____

____

____

____

18. Take into consideration the power of rituals and ceremonies that celebrate and honor your self-acceptance and self-love. How can you use these practices to mark your journey towards empowerment?

____
____
____
____
____
____
____
____
____
____

19. Inspect the role of community and support in your self-acceptance and self-love. How can you connect with like-minded individuals who understand and encourage your path and self-acceptance?

____
____
____
____
____
____
____
____
____
____

20. Finally, think on the concept of self-acceptance as the foundation for all magical and spiritual work. How can you build a strong sense of self-love and self-acceptance that empowers your practice   as   a   witch?

____
____
____
____
____
____
____
____
____

Chapter 26

Breaking the Chains

1. Review your earliest memories of addictive behaviors or self-destructive patterns. How have these early experiences influenced your current struggles with addiction as a witch?

____
____
____
____
____
____
____
____
____
____

2. Brainstorm on the influence of societal norms and pressures on your addictive behaviors and self-sabotage. How can you challenge these influences to make healthier choices for your well-being?

____
____
____
____
____
____
____
____
____
____

3. Call to mind any fears or anxieties you have related to confronting your addictions or self-destructive habits. How can you work on transforming these fears into a source of motivation for recovery?

____
____
____
____

4. Integrate the connection between addiction and spirituality. How can your magical and spiritual beliefs support your journey toward healing and recovery?

5. Give thought to the role of self-compassion and self-care in addiction recovery. How can you prioritize self-compassion in your daily life as a witch to foster recovery?

6. Touch upon the impact of past traumas and emotional wounds on your addictive behaviors and self-sabotage. How can you use your magical practice to heal and release these wounds?

7. Interpret the symbolism of transformation and rebirth in your magical work. How can you use these symbols to empower your journey of recovery and healing?

8. Research the concept of protection spells and rituals as tools for safeguarding your well-being and maintaining sobriety. How can you create a shield of strength to ward off relapse triggers?

9. Look into the influence of shadow work in addressing the deeper emotional issues that contribute to addiction and self-sabotage. How can you use shadow work to confront and transform these underlying wounds?

10. Incorporate the role of vulnerability and authenticity in addiction recovery. How can you embrace your true self and share your struggles openly without fear of judgment?

____

____

____

____

____

____

____

____

____

11. Review the idea of mindfulness and meditation as a means of maintaining sobriety and self-awareness. How can you use these practices to stay grounded and connected to your inner strength?

____

____

____

____

____

____

____

____

____

12. Weigh the use of grounding techniques and earth-centered rituals to help you stay connected to your path of recovery. How can you use the stability of the Earth to support your healing?

____

____

____

____

____

____

____

____

____

____

13. Bring to mind the power of community and support in addiction recovery. How can you connect with like-minded individuals who understand and encourage your journey to heal and recover?

____

____

____

____

____

____

____

____

____

____

14. Look into the concept of releasing old patterns and habits through ritual and ceremony. How can you use these practices to symbolize your commitment to letting go of self-destructive behaviors?

____

____

____

____

____

____

____

____

15. Be curious about the role of self-discipline and accountability in maintaining sobriety. How can you use your magical practice to strengthen your resolve and commitment to recovery?

16. Call upon the symbolism of herbs, crystals, and elements in your healing rituals and recovery journey. How can you harness these allies to support your well-being and sobriety?

17. Explore the idea of self-forgiveness and self-love as crucial components of addiction recovery. How can you release guilt and shame and cultivate a more compassionate relationship with yourself?

18. Meditate on the use of divination, tarot or oracle cards for example, to gain insights into your addiction and recovery path. How can you use divination to guide your decision-making and healing process?

____

____

____

____

____

____

____

____

____

____

____

19. Give some thought to the role of ritual baths and cleansing practices in releasing old energy and attachments related to addiction. How can you purify your spirit and embrace a fresh start?

____

____

____

____

____

____

____

____

____

____

20. Finally, don't forget that the concept of sobriety can be seen as a sacred journey and a powerful form of self-transformation. How can you use your magical practice to celebrate and honor your ongoing recovery and healing?

____

____

____

Chapter 27

Embracing the Spiral of Life

1. Meditate on your earliest memories of encountering the concept of aging and death. How have these early experiences shaped your beliefs and fears as a witch?

____
____
____
____
____
____
____
____
____
____

2. Take into account your fears related to physical aging. How can you work on transforming these fears into a source of wisdom, growth, and acceptance of the natural life cycle?

____
____
____
____
____
____
____
____
____
____

3. Discuss the influence of societal attitudes and beauty standards on your anxieties about aging. How can you challenge these influences to celebrate the beauty of the aging process?

____
____
____
____
____
____

____

____

____

____

4. Assess your spiritual beliefs and how they intersect with the concepts of aging and mortality. How can your magical and spiritual path provide guidance and solace in the face of death?

____

____

____

____

____

____

____

____

____

____

5. Investigate the symbolism of the cycles of life, death, and rebirth in your magical work. How can you use these symbols to foster a deeper understanding and acceptance of mortality?

____

____

____

____

____

____

____

____

____

____

6. Think about the impact of ancestral wisdom and traditions on your views of aging and mortality. How can you honor and learn from these ancestral influences to navigate your own aging process?

____

____

____

____

____

____

____

____

____

____

____

7. Review your relationships with elders and the elderly. How can you connect with and learn from the wisdom of older generations as a means of embracing your own aging journey?

____

____

____

____

____

____

____

____

____

____

8. Take into account the concept of end-of-life rituals and ceremonies as tools for facing mortality. How can you use these practices to prepare for and celebrate the transition into the next   phase   of   existence?

____

____

____

____

____

____

____

____

____

____

9. Examine the influence of meditative and reflective practices in fostering a deeper understanding of mortality. How can these practices help you come to terms with the impermanence   of   life?

____

____

10. Journey into the role of shadow work in addressing your fears and anxieties related to aging and death. How can you use shadow work to confront and transform these deep-seated concerns?

11. Give thought to the idea of embracing the present moment and living mindfully as a means of transcending fear of aging and death. How can you cultivate a sense of gratitude for the now?

12. Deliberate on the symbolism of the moon and its phases in your magical work. How can the moon's cyclical nature inspire you to accept the natural cycles of life and death?

13. Dig into the role of community and support in facing the aging process. How can you connect with like-minded individuals who understand and encourage your journey toward acceptance?

14. Check out the concept of death as a form of transformation and renewal in your magical practice. How can you use this perspective to find beauty and purpose in the cycle of life and death?

15. Consider the use of protective and boundary-setting spells to navigate your fears of mortality and protect your sense of safety and well-being.

____
____
____
____
____
____
____
____
____
____

16. Analyze the power of divination and communication with ancestors as a means of gaining insights and guidance regarding aging and death. How can you connect with ancestral wisdom for your journey?

____
____
____
____
____
____
____
____
____
____

17. Determine the concept of legacy and the lasting impact you want to leave behind as a witch. How can you work on creating a meaningful legacy as a way to transcend the fear of death?

____
____
____
____
____
____
____
____
____

18. Study the use of herbal and plant magic to help you find solace and healing during your shadow work on aging and mortality. How can these natural allies support your journey?

____

____

____

____

____

____

____

____

____

19. Dive into the symbolism of the phoenix and its cycle of death and rebirth in your magical practice. How can you use this symbolism to find strength and resilience in the face of mortality?

____

____

____

____

____

____

____

____

____

____

20. Finally, take into account the concept of embracing your aging and mortality as a natural and sacred part of your life journey. How can you use your magical practice to celebrate and honor the wisdom and experience that come with age?

____

____

____

____

____

____

____

Chapter 28

Dreamscapes and Vision Work

1. Give thought to your earliest dreams and aspirations. How have these early aspirations influenced your current desires and goals as a witch?

____
____
____
____
____
____
____
____
____

2. Inspect any fears or doubts that have held you back from pursuing your dreams and aspirations. How can you work on transforming these fears into sources of motivation and empowerment?

____
____
____
____
____
____
____
____
____
____

3. Look into the influence of societal expectations and external pressures on your dreams and goals. How can you challenge these influences to create authentic and fulfilling aspirations?

____
____
____
____
____

____

____

____

____

____

4. Inquire about the connection between your dreams and your magical and spiritual path. How can your spiritual beliefs and practices support your journey toward manifesting your desires?

____

____

____

____

____

____

____

____

____

____

5. Examine the symbolism of intention-setting and manifestation in your magical work. How can you use your magical practice to set clear intentions and manifest your dreams into reality?

____

____

____

____

____

____

____

____

____

6. Check out the use of divination using tarot or oracle cards as tools for gaining insights into your dreams and aspirations. How can you use divination to guide your decision-making and goal-setting
                                                            process?

____

____

____

7. Meditate on the role of affirmations and positive intentions in achieving your dreams. How can you use these tools to reframe your beliefs and cultivate a mindset of empowerment and success?

____

____

____

____

____

____

____

____

____

____

____

8. Look into the idea of creating vision boards and visualization practices to manifest your aspirations. How can you use these practices to amplify your intentions and bring your desires to   life?

____

____

____

____

____

____

____

____

____

____

____

9. Look into the influence of shadow work in addressing any limiting beliefs and self-sabotage that may hinder your progress toward your dreams and aspirations. How can you use shadow work to confront and transform these barriers?

10. Investigate the symbolism of the elements and their connection to your dreams and goals. How can you align your aspirations with the elemental energies that resonate with your path?

11. Question the concept of dream journals and recording your experiences as a means of uncovering deeper desires and understanding your true aspirations.

12. Imagine using the moons magic and lunar phases to support your goal-setting and intention manifestation. How can you harness the moon's energy to amplify your dreams?

____

____

____

____

____

____

____

____

____

13. Take into consideration the role of self-discipline and time management in pursuing your aspirations. How can you use your magical practice to enhance your focus and productivity?

____

____

____

____

____

____

____

____

____

____

14. Be curious about the concept of co-creating with the universe and synchronicity in achieving your dreams. How can you recognize and seize opportunities that align with your aspirations?

____

____

____

____

____

____

____

____

____

15. Recall the influence of divinely guided dreams and messages in your life. How can you interpret and act upon these spiritual insights to manifest your desires?

____
____
____
____
____
____
____
____
____
____

16. Take a closer look at your role as a creator and manifestor within your magical and spiritual path. How can you embrace your power to shape your own reality and bring your dreams to fruition?

____
____
____
____
____
____
____
____
____
____

17. Uncover the idea of aligning your dreams and aspirations with your values and spiritual purpose. How can you ensure that your goals are in harmony with your deeper spiritual path?

____
____
____
____
____
____
____
____
____
____

18. Research the use of crystal and herbal magic to enhance your intention-setting and manifestation practices. How can these magical allies amplify your efforts to manifest your desires?

____

____

____

____

____

____

____

____

____

19. Go over the concept of perseverance and determination in achieving your dreams. How can you stay committed to your path and overcome obstacles along the way?

____

____

____

____

____

____

____

____

____

____

20. Finally, inquire about the concept of gratitude and celebration in acknowledging your achievements and the realization of your dreams and aspirations. How can you use your magical practice to express gratitude and continue to create the life you desire?

____

____

____

____

____

____

____

Chapter 29

Detox Your Digital Shadow

1. Remember your earliest memories with technology and its role in your life. How have these early experiences influenced your relationship with screens and the digital world as a witch?

____
____
____
____
____
____
____
____
____
____

2. Check on any fears or anxieties related to the overuse of technology and digital devices. How can you work on transforming these fears into a source of motivation for a digital detox?

____
____
____
____
____
____
____
____
____
____
____

3. Observe the influence of societal norms and screen addiction on your technology habits. How can you challenge these influences to regain control over your digital life?

____
____
____
____
____
____
____

4. Feel out the connection between your magical and spiritual path and your digital habits. How can your spiritual beliefs support your journey toward finding balance in the digital age?

5. Review the symbolism of balance and moderation in your magical work. How can you use your magical practice to strike a harmonious equilibrium between the digital and tangible worlds?

6. Look into the impact of overexposure to screens on your mental and emotional well-being. How can you use your magical practice to foster a more mindful and balanced relationship with technology?

7. Weigh in on the role of digital detox rituals and ceremonies in reclaiming your connection to the tangible world. How can you use these practices to signify your intention to limit screen time?

8. Investigate into the concept of grounding and reconnecting with nature as a means of finding balance in the digital world. How can you use nature-based practices to restore your connection with the Earth?

9. Acknowledge the influence of shadow work in addressing the deeper emotional issues that may drive excessive screen use. How can you use shadow work to confront and transform these underlying emotional triggers?

10. Take into consideration the symbolism of the elements and their connection to your technology detox. How can you align your intention to disconnect from screens with the elemental energies that resonate with your path?

11. Take a dive into the idea of setting digital boundaries and using protective spells to maintain your screen-free time. How can you create a magical shield to protect your boundaries from external pressures?

12. Research the use of mindfulness and meditation to regain focus and presence in your everyday life. How can you use these practices to reduce screen time and be more attentive to the   tangible   world?

____

____

____

____

____

____

____

____

____

13. Recall your relationships and how they are affected by technology use. How can you foster deeper connections with others by being more present and engaged in the moment?

____

____

____

____

____

____

____

____

____

____

14. Question the concept of unplugging and practicing digital fasting as a way to reset your relationship with screens. How can you use these practices to cleanse your digital presence?

____

____

____

____

____

____

____

____

____

____

15. Integrate the influence of dreams and dream work in revealing your deep-seated fears and desires related to technology and the digital world. How can you use dream interpretation to gain insights into your digital detox journey?

____
____
____
____
____
____
____
____
____
____

16. Look into your role of self-discipline and willpower in maintaining a digital detox. How can you use your magical practice to strengthen your resolve and stay committed to your screen-time limits?

____
____
____
____
____
____
____
____
____
____

17. Take a closer look at the idea of creating screen-free sacred spaces in your home. How can you use these spaces to reconnect with your spiritual path and the tangible world around you?

____
____
____
____
____
____
____

18. Weigh the use of crystal and herbal magic to enhance your digital detox and mindfulness practices. How can these magical allies amplify your efforts to reduce screen time?

19. Go over the concept of rediscovering hobbies and passions that do not involve screens. How can you use these activities to enrich your life and find joy in the tangible world?

20. Finally, look into the concept of gratitude and appreciation for the tangible world and the present moment. How can you use your magical practice to express gratitude for the simple pleasures and experiences that exist beyond the digital realm?

Chapter 30

Secrets of the Labyrinth

1. Describe some recurring symbols or signs that have appeared in your dreams? Explain them here   in   detail.

____

____

____

____

____

____

____

____

____

____

2. Remember any symbols or signs you've encountered in your daily life. Are there patterns in when   and   where   they   appear?

____

____

____

____

____

____

____

____

____

____

____

____

3. Have you ever experienced synchronicities or meaningful coincidences involving specific symbols   or   signs?   Share   those   experiences.

____

____

____

____

____

____

4. Research the symbolism of any animals that have crossed your path repeatedly. What do they represent in your life?

____

____

____

____

____

____

____

____

____

5. Connect with any celestial signs you've experienced, like shooting stars, rainbows, or lunar phases. How might they relate to your inner journey?

____

____

____

____

____

____

____

____

____

6. Study any recurring numbers that catch your attention. What significance do these numbers hold for you, and how might they connect to your shadow self?

____

____

____

____

____

7. Have you encountered specific plants or flowers that seem to appear consistently in your life? Explore their mystical meanings and any emotional associations.

8. Aknowledge any recurring weather patterns or natural elements (e.g., thunderstorms, rain, wind) and how they might mirror your inner emotional landscape.

9. Look into any symbols or signs that remind you of your ancestral heritage. What role might they play in your shadow work?

10. Take into consideration your experiences with déjà vu. When and where have you felt like you've encountered a moment or place before?

11. Think about any symbols or signs that hold personal significance. What stories or memories are associated with them?

12. Have you ran into any specific colors or combinations of colors that seem to reappear in your life? What emotions do they evoke?

13. Analyze your experiences with sacred geometry, like mandalas or geometric patterns. How might they connect with your spiritual and shadow journey?

14. Take into account any experiences with mirror symbolism. When have you felt a profound connection to your reflection or a sense of duality?

15. Look into any recurring dreams of water, such as oceans, rivers, or lakes. What emotions and themes are present in these dreams?

16. Find any symbols or signs related to protection, such as amulets or talismans. How have they influenced your feelings of safety and security?

17. Question any symbols or signs that relate to divination tools like tarot cards, runes, or pendulums. How have they guided your introspection?

18. Inspect the symbols that you associate with deities, archetypes, or spiritual figures. How do they manifest in your life and shadow work?

19. Review your experiences with signs of transformation, such as butterflies, snakes, or other creatures that undergo metamorphosis.

20. Brainstorm on the idea of sacred space and places. Are there specific locations or environments where you've encountered meaningful symbols or signs?

Chapter 31

From Shadow to Light

1. Call to mind the most significant insights gained from your shadow work journey. How have these revelations transformed your perspective on life?

____
____
____
____
____
____
____
____
____
____

2. Identify a specific shadow aspect that you've worked on. Describe the practical steps you've taken to integrate the lessons learned into your daily life.

____
____
____
____
____
____
____
____
____
____

3. Share a ritual or technique that has helped you manifest positive change as a result of your shadow work. How has it influenced your transformation?

____
____
____
____
____
____

____

____

____

____

____

4. Give thought to how your shadow work has affected your relationships. Have you noticed any changes in your interactions with others as you've integrated your shadow self?

____

____

____

____

____

____

____

____

____

5. Outline a personal growth milestone you've achieved through shadow work. How did you reach this point, and what are your next steps?

____

____

____

____

____

____

____

____

____

6. Inspect your daily routines and habits. How have you altered them to align with the insights gained from your shadow work?

____

____

____

____

7. Share a creative expression, artwork, or writing that represents your journey of integration and transformation.

8. Investigate the role of gratitude in your shadow work journey. How has embracing gratitude impacted your life and personal growth?

9. Talk about a significant dream or vision experienced during your shadow work that has guided your path of integration and transformation.

10. How have you harnessed the energy of a specific crystal or herb to aid in your integration process? Share your experiences and any rituals you've created.

11. Address moments when you faced resistance in integrating shadow work insights. What strategies have helped you overcome such resistance?

12. Describe a daily affirmation or mantra that empowers your journey of self-discovery and integration.

____

____

____

____

____

____

____

____

13. Speak about a story or example of a moment when you felt a profound sense of empowerment due to your shadow work.

____

____

____

____

____

____

____

____

____

____

14. Discuss the role of community or support networks in your shadow work journey. How have they contributed to your integration and transformation?

____

____

____

____

____

____

____

____

____

____

15. Meditate on a symbol or sign encountered in your life that seems directly connected to your shadow work. What message or lesson does it hold for you?

____

____

____

16. Touch upon the concept of forgiveness as a part of the integration process. How has forgiving yourself or others played a role in your transformation?

____

17. Share a self-care ritual or practice that has become essential to your integration and personal growth.

____

18. Think over the theme of balancing the light and shadow aspects of yourself. How have you found equilibrium, and what have you learned in the process?

19. Identify a moment of synchronicity that occurred during your journey of integration and transformation. How did it impact your path?

20. Demonstrate your aspirations and intentions for the future as a result of your shadow work journey. How do you plan to continue your pursuit of self-discovery and empowerment?

Chapter 32

Balancing Shadows

1. Self-Acceptance, Self-Love & Self-Worth: One of the first steps you can take is to accept that your shadow is an integral part of who you are. You need to understand that it contains both your challenges and your strengths. By acknowledging this, you can start to see the value in exploring and integrating your shadow.

2. Mindfulness: Practice mindfulness to stay present with your emotions, thoughts, and reactions. This awareness is crucial for recognizing when shadow aspects surface. Being mindful of your emotional and mental states can help you understand when you are projecting your shadow onto others or when you are triggered by someone else's shadow.

3. Journaling: Maintaining a shadow work journal can be helpful in documenting your discoveries and reflections. This practice helps you track your progress and identify patterns. By writing down your thoughts and feelings, you can gain clarity on your shadow aspects and identify any recurring themes or patterns that need attention.

4. Emotional Expression: It's essential to allow yourself to feel and express your emotions. Avoid repressing or denying them, as they often hold the keys to your shadow aspects. By expressing your emotions in a healthy way, you can release any pent-up feelings that may be holding you back from integrating your shadow.

5. Therapy or Counseling: Consider seeking professional support to delve deeper into your shadow work. Therapists and counselors can provide guidance and tools for healing. **If you're grappling with severe depression or experiencing suicidal thoughts, it's essential to seek immediate help from a trained therapist or mental health professional. (988 Suicide and Crisis Lifeline - USA)** Your mental and emotional well-being is of the highest importance, and reaching out to a therapist is a crucial step toward healing and finding a path to recovery. **Please, don't hesitate to seek professional assistance—it can make a life saving difference.** Therapists and counselors can provide guidance and tools for healing, and they can help you navigate the complexity of incorporating your shadow.

Healing your Shadow:

When it comes to healing your shadow aspects, there are several techniques and practices that you can utilize. The following are some effective ones:

1. Energy Work: Practices like Reiki, energy healing, and aura cleansing can be instrumental in releasing trapped emotions and restoring energetic balance. These practices aim to remove any blockages in your energy field and help you feel more aligned and balanced. **Example:** Practice

Reiki by placing your hands over areas with discomfort, visualizing healing energy flow, and intending the release of emotional blockages.

2. Chakra Balancing: The chakra system represents various aspects of your being. Balancing your chakras can help align your mind, body, and spirit, promoting overall well-being. You can balance your chakras using various techniques, including meditation, visualization, and energy work. **Example:** Meditate on each chakra, envisioning a spinning wheel of light. For the root chakra, focus on stability and security, promoting overall well-being.

3. Meditation: Regular meditation sessions can help you connect with your inner self, confront shadow aspects, and cultivate inner peace. By meditating regularly, you can develop a sense of calm and clarity that can help you navigate your shadow aspects with greater ease. **Example:** Sit comfortably, focus on your breath, and observe thoughts without attachment. Regular sessions cultivate calmness and clarity for navigating shadow aspects.

4. Visualization: Use guided visualizations to explore and heal specific shadow aspects. Visualization can be a powerful way to reframe and transform these aspects. By visualizing yourself in a different light, you can begin to shift your perspective and open up to new possibilities. **Example:** Use guided visualizations to reframe and transform shadow aspects. Visualize a bright light dissolving a dark cloud, shifting your perspective.

5. Inner Child Work: Addressing and healing your inner child's wounds can be a profound aspect of shadow work. Techniques like inner child meditations and dialogues can be helpful in accessing and healing these wounds. **Example:** Practice inner child meditations by imagining comforting and talking to your younger self, addressing past experiences with compassion and understanding.

6. Dreamwork: Pay attention to your dreams and utilize dream analysis techniques to interpret and work through your shadow's messages. Dreams can offer valuable insights into your subconscious mind and can help you uncover hidden aspects of your shadow. **Example:** Keep a dream journal, noting recurring themes to uncover hidden aspects. Also, in your journal use the templates listed in chapter 10.

7. Crystal Healing: Crystals and gemstones can aid in your healing journey. Choose stones with energies that resonate with your specific shadow aspects. By working with crystals, you can harness their energies to support your healing and transformation. **Example:** Choose crystals resonating with specific shadow aspects. Use amethyst for clarity; hold it during meditation, visualizing its energy releasing and transforming negative patterns. Use the knowledge learned in chapter 12 to choose a crystal that resonates with you and your personal shadow work journey.

8. Sound Therapy: Sound healing, including techniques like using singing bowls or binaural beats, can help release emotional blockages and promote healing. **Example:** Listen to singing bowls or binaural beats to release emotional blockages. Allow the resonant tones to penetrate and harmonize your energetic system.

9. Affirmations: Develop positive affirmations that address your shadow aspects. Repeating these affirmations can gradually rewire your thought patterns. By affirming positive beliefs about yourself, you can begin to shift your perspective and cultivate greater self-love and acceptance. **Example:** Develop positive affirmations addressing shadow aspects. Repeat "I am worthy and deserving" to rewire thought patterns and enhance self-love

10. Rituals and Spells: Craft spells or rituals that are specific to your shadow work. These can serve as symbolic actions that aid in transformation and healing. By creating rituals that are meaningful to you, you can tap into the power of intention and create a space for healing and growth. **Example:** Craft symbolic rituals such as lighting a candle, symbolizing illumination and intention, creating a sacred space for healing and growth.

By combining these strategies for inclusion and healing on your shadow work expedition, you can nurture a deeper awareness of yourself, be able to address past wounds, and set out on a path of profound self-help and autonomy.

Chapter 33

Respecting the Shadows

The practice of witchcraft, like any other spiritual or religious path, comes with its own set of ethical considerations that you must be mindful of. Here are some common ethical principles:

1. Respect for Free Will: A fundamental tenet of ethical witchcraft is the respect for free will. This means that you should never use your magical abilities to manipulate or control the thoughts, feelings, or actions of others without their consent. Informed consent and respect for individual choices are paramount.

2. Continuous Self-Reflection: Like in any practice, ongoing self-reflection and growth are crucial. You can engage in self-examination to ensure your magical work aligns with your own values. This will help you identify any biases or assumptions that may be impacting your work and allows you to adjust your practices accordingly.

3. Responsibility: You are encouraged to take responsibility for your actions and their impact on the world. This includes acknowledging and rectifying any unintended harm or consequences that may arise from youir magical workings. Remember to be mindful of the potential consequences of your actions and take steps to mitigate any negative impacts.

4. Confidentiality: Respecting the privacy and confidentiality of others is essential in ethical witchcraft. Information shared in the context of magical or spiritual work should be kept confidential unless consent to share is given. Please be mindful of the power dynamics at play and ensure that you are not exploiting your knowledge or influence for personal gain.

5. Environmental Care: You may feel a deep connection to the Earth and place a strong emphasis on environmental sustainability and responsible resource use. You might engage in practices aimed at protecting and preserving the natural world. Possibly try to work to reduce your ecological footprint and engage in activism or advocacy for environmental causes.

6. Cultural Sensitivity: Remember to be mindful of cultural appropriation, acknowledging the origins and significance of the traditions they draw from. It's important to avoid misrepresenting or misusing cultural practices. Be respectful of the cultural roots of your practices and work to ensure that they are not perpetuating harmful stereotypes or engaging in cultural appropriation.

7. Self-Improvement and Limitless Learning: Ethical witchcraft often involves ongoing self-reflection and learning. You may strive to develop a deeper understanding of yourself and your motivations to ensure your magical work aligns with your values and principles. This involves an ongoing commitment to self-improvement and ongoing education.

8. Non-Discrimination: It's very important to emphasize the magnitude of non-discrimination and inclusivity. Witchcraft is open to all, regardless of gender, race, sexual orientation, or any other characteristic. It invites you to explore your unique path and discover your own spiritual truths. The beauty of witchcraft is that it is a spiritual practice that can be tailored to suit the needs, beliefs, and backgrounds of anyone who feels drawn to it.

9. Harm Reduction: Harm reduction is an important aspect of ethical witchcraft, and you may use your magical abilities to promote healing and reduce harm in the world. This could involve spellwork aimed at reducing violence or promoting emotional healing, and it can be a powerful way for you to contribute to a more positive change in the natural world.

10. Personal Sovereignty: Personal sovereignty is a central value in ethical witchcraft, and you know that every person has the right to make their own decisions about their life and spiritual practices. Remember to respect others' personal sovereignty and avoid imposing your beliefs or practices on others without consent, creating a safe and inclusive space for all.

Chapter 34

The Light Within

In my final moments with you, I want to convey a message of freedom, self-appreciation, and the everlasting nature of your spiritual expedition.

As you come to the end of your travels here, remember that you have now discovered the fierce power inside yourself, with self-love, and knowing just how strong you really are. Through your search into the depths of your shadow self, you have faced your fears and hurdled over challenges, and resurfaced as a more aware, resilient, and substantial version of yourself. Your shadow is not something to be feared but rather a source of hidden wisdom and strength.

As you continue on your journey, remember that loving your whole self, flaws and all, is the true essence of witchcraft. It's about finding your inner balance and living authentically, forging a deeper connection with your own strength. The integration of your shadow self, with all its complexities, is your ticket to a beautiful life.

Take these lessons with you: honor your past, your fears, your desires, and your shadow. Remember that the practice of shadow work is not a destination but an ongoing, circular process. Embrace it with love, compassion, and a sense of wonder, for it is your unique path in your life.

May your days be filled with the light of self-love and the warmth of self-worth. Continue your craft with an open heart to the the universe and the wisdom of your shadow. You are the master of your own evolution. Embrace the shadows, and may your path be illuminated by the magic of wisdom.

Chapter 35

Witches Shadows Unveiled FAQ'S

1.What is Witches Shadow Work?

Witches shadow work, rooted in spiritual and magical traditions, digs into heart-felt inward analysis and personal progress. Drawing from the dogma of Swiss psychiatrist Carl Jung, this developmental training unfolds through some key points:

-Self-Awareness: At its core, witch's shadow work prompts deep self-awareness, urging you to survey beyond your visible personas. This inward survey unveils buried, denied, or overlooked aspects of your personality, emotions, and experiences, fostering a profound self-realization.

-The Shadow: From Jungian psychology, the concept of "the shadow" encapsulates unconscious aspects like fears, insecurities, desires, and unresolved traumas. Witch's shadow work integrates this concept into spiritual and magical practices, recognizing the importance of addressing hidden layers. While the shadow is an important archetype in Jungian psychology, Carl Jung introduces twelve archetypes that illuminate the diverse characters of the human psyche. These archetypes, ranging from the Hero to the Jester, offer a comprehensive framework for understanding the complexities inherent in personal and spiritual exploration.

-Healing and Integration: Your intention is to elevate the shadow into conscious awareness and employ diverse techniques for healing and integration. By acknowledging and embracing these veiled aspects, you can strive for a more balanced and holistic self, breaking through sensitive barriers.

-Personal Growth: Your ultimate aspiration is personal improvement and independence. By confronting and processing shadow elements, you can undergo a metamorphic experience, fostering increased self-confidence, emotional resilience, and a clearer sense of your life's purpose.

-Magical and Ritual Elements: Witches shadow work embodies magical practices such as meditation, journaling, dream analysis, divination, spellwork, and guided visualizations. These rituals provide a spiritual context for exploring and addressing your shadow and it helps create a more dynamic and interconnected adventure.

-Community and Support: Whether pursued individually or within a group or coven, witch's shadow work can be emotionally challenging. Support from experienced practitioners or mentors becomes pivotal, fostering a sense of community and guidance during this introspective journey.

It is crucial to acknowledge that witches shadow work is deeply personal, defying a one-size-fits-all approach. Your unique experience and ongoing processes contribute to a powerful instrument for personal revision. The goal is not eradication of your shadow, but conscious integration, making your shadow a sympathetic component of the entirety of self.

2. How does witches shadow work differ from traditional shadow work?

Witches shadow work, as a specific subset of traditional shadow work, incorporates the principles, beliefs, and practices of witchcraft and magic to explore and heal one's shadow self.

-Incorporation of Magical and Witchcraft Practices: Witches shadow work distinguishes itself by seamlessly integrating magical and witchcraft practices into the exploration and healing of your shadow self. This involves utilizing spells, rituals, and various magical techniques as influential tools for improving the effectiveness of your shadow work process.

-Use of Rituals: Rituals play a central role in witches shadow work, serving as meaningful ceremonies designed to address and transform your shadow aspects. You may invoke deities or spirits, establish sacred spaces, and employ magical tools such as candles, herbs, crystals, and talismans to facilitate a deeply immersive and transformative shadow work experience.

-Spells and Incantations: Spellwork becomes an essential component, allowing you to craft spells focused on revealing hidden emotions, healing past traumas, and empowering yourself to confront and integrate your shadow aspects. Incantations and affirmations are harnessed as powerful tools for reprogramming negative beliefs and thoughts.

-Connection to Nature and the Elements: You may weave a strong connection to nature and the elements into your shadow work. Aligning with natural cycles, such as the moon phases or changing seasons, enhances the understanding and transformation of shadow aspects. This connection emphasizes your harmony with the larger universe.

-Sacred Symbols and Tools: Witches shadow work employs sacred symbols and tools that are notable in some witchcraft traditions. These symbols, like the pentacle representing the five elements, serve as conduits to work with specific phases of the shadow self, infusing the exploration with deep meaning.

-Deity and Spirit Work: You may incorporate deity and spirit work into your shadow exploration. Invoking or working with deities, spirits, or ancestors can provide deeper guidance and assistance in addressing and healing shadow aspects, helping you to foster a deeper spiritual connection.

-Energetic and Psychic Practices: Your shadow work may involve energetic practices, such as energy clearing, chakra work, or psychic development. These practices deepen insights into shadow aspects, facilitating healing at an energetic level and creating a more comprehensive approach to self-discovery.

-Holistic Approach: Taking a holistic view, your shadow work considers the self as interconnected with the universe. This approach addresses not only individual psychological aspects but also acknowledges your interconnectedness with the spiritual and natural world, fostering a sense of unity.

-Alignment with Spiritual Beliefs: Your shadow work can align seamlessly with the spiritual beliefs and perspectives of witchcraft. Embracing the principles of duality in nature and acknowledging the interconnectedness of all things are integral to navigating the witches shadow work journey. These foundational concepts form a guiding compass for your transformative exploration.

In essence, witches shadow work emerges as a specialized and deeply personalized form of traditional shadow work, enriched by the infusion of magical practices and an esoteric alignment with the spiritual beliefs inherent in witchcraft and magic.

3. Why is shadow work important in witchcraft?

Witches shadow work holds distinct significance within the realm of witchcraft, sharing principles with traditional shadow work while introducing specialized methodologies deeply rooted in magical practices:

-Incorporation of Witchcraft and Magic: Witches shadow work distinguishes itself by weaving witchcraft and magical practices into the exploration of the shadow self. This specialized form of shadow work involves rituals, spells, divination, and other magical techniques not typically employed in traditional approaches. These mystical elements elevate the process beyond psychological exploration, providing a dynamic and spiritually charged context.

-Rituals and Spells: Central to your shadow work is personalized rituals and spells crafted to explore and heal your shadow. They often involve symbolic elements such as candles, herbs, crystals, and magical tools, creating a evolutionary environment that surpasses traditional therapeutic approaches. The incorporation of symbolism and magical tools enhances the symbolic and ritualistic dimensions of your process.

-Archetypal and Mythological Elements: This particular approach helps you incorporate archetypal and mythological elements derived from your magical traditions. You may engage with specific deities, spirits, or mythological narratives that resonate with your shadow aspects, adding a layer of symbolic depth that is absent in traditional shadow work. This focus extends beyond individual psychology to embrace archetypal and mythological symbolism.

-Empowerment and Spiritual Growth: Beyond self-awareness and healing, your shadow work will be aiming at personal and spiritual empowerment within your magical and witchcraft traditions. It contains the improvement of your magical abilities, a deeper connection to the spiritual realm, and progression along your spiritual path. This spiritual and magical dimension sets witch's shadow work apart from traditional approaches, which may lack these explicit goals.

In essence, witches shadow work emerges as a specialized, spiritually charged exploration of the shadow self, complementing traditional psychological methods with the developmental power of magical practices. The choice between these approaches often hinges on individual beliefs, goals, and preferences, allowing you to align with the method that resonates most profoundly with your personal self.

4. What tools or rituals can enhance a witches shadow work?:

-Candles: Candles serve as essential tools, chosen for their symbolic significance. Different colors represent various facets of the self or emotions under scrutiny. Lighting candles establishes a focused and sacred ambiance, fostering self-reflection and meditation within the witch's shadow work rituals.

-Crystals: Crystals, renowned for their energetic properties, play an important role. Each crystal is chosen purposefully; for instance, amethyst aids in healing and clarity, while obsidian is linked to protection and shadow confrontation. Crystals can be held, worn, or arranged on altars during rituals, infusing the environment with their unique energies.

-Herbs: Herbs contribute versatile elements to witch's shadow work, whether through incense, herbal teas, or spell sachets. Mugwort, sage, and lavender, among others, are harnessed for purification and heightened psychic awareness. Integration into rituals enhances the magical and spiritually attuned ambiance.

-Tarot Cards: Tarot cards emerge as potent tools for self-reflection and divination during shadow work. Specially designed spreads aid in exploring the inner world, gaining insights into hidden aspects, and identifying areas requiring healing. Each card within the tarot deck carries symbolic significance, resonating with different facets of the shadow.

-Meditation: Meditation stands as a foundational practice in witches shadow work. Through guided meditations tailored to shadow exploration, individuals quiet the mind, delve within, and establish a profound connection with their deeper selves. It provides a safe and controlled avenue for engaging with shadow aspects.

-Journaling: Keeping a shadow work journal proves invaluable. This practice involves documenting thoughts, emotions, dreams, and insights, aiding in progress tracking and gaining clarity about shadow aspects. Journaling also serves as a therapeutic outlet for expressing challenging emotions.

-Visualization: Visualization techniques become powerful tools for confronting and working with shadow aspects in the imagination. Practitioners may visualize facing their shadows, engaging in conversations with them, or envisioning transformation into more positive and integrated aspects of the self.

-Rituals and Spellwork: Witches shadow work often entails specific rituals and spellwork, uniquely crafted to address and heal shadow aspects. Personalized rituals may incorporate symbols, chants, and other magical techniques, acting as catalysts for transformation and integration.

- Altar: Maintaining a dedicated shadow work altar proves common among witches. Adorned with relevant symbols, crystals, candles, and other items representing the journey of self-discovery and healing, the altar becomes a focal point for their practice.

-Ancestral Work: Ancestral work finds a place within some witches shadow work. This involves connecting with ancestors for guidance and support in the shadow work process, as well as acknowledging and healing ancestral wounds.

It's essential to recognize that the choice of tools and rituals in witches shadow work is highly individualized, varying based on beliefs, preferences, and specific shadow work goals. The overarching objective is to create a sacred and focused space conducive to inner exploration and transformation, honoring your unique journey.

5. How do I know if I need to do shadow work?

Knowing whether you need to do shadow work is a deeply personal and introspective process. It involves self-reflection and an awareness of your emotional and psychological state. Here are some key signs that may suggest you might benefit from participating in shadow work:

-Desire for Personal Growth: One of the primary motivations for shadow work is a genuine desire for personal growth and self-improvement. If you're looking to understand yourself better, evolve as an individual, and become more self-aware, shadow work can be a valuable tool in your journey.

-Unresolved Emotional Issues: If you have unresolved emotional issues from your past that continue to impact your present life and well-being, this is a strong indicator that shadow work could be beneficial. The shadow often contains repressed emotions, traumas, and aspects of ourselves that we haven't fully acknowledged or processed.

-Feeling Stuck or Blocked: If you find yourself feeling stuck or blocked in various aspects of your life, such as relationships, career, or personal goals, it may be a sign that unresolved issues and internal conflicts are holding you back. Shadow work can help you identify and address these barriers.

-Recurring Negative Patterns: If you notice that you keep repeating negative patterns in your life, such as self-sabotage, destructive behaviors, or toxic relationships, it's an indication that there may be underlying shadow aspects at play. Shadow work can help you identify and transform these patterns.

-**Emotional Turmoil:** If you frequently experience intense and unexplained emotional turmoil, such as anger, fear, or sadness, it may be a sign that your shadow is attempting to communicate with you. These emotions can be a signal that unresolved issues are seeking your attention.

-**Inconsistencies in Self-Image:** If you have inconsistencies in how you perceive yourself, such as feeling confident in certain areas of your life but insecure in others, it may suggest that you are not fully aware of all aspects of your self-image. Shadow work can help you reconcile these inconsistencies.

-**Dreams and Nightmares:** Paying attention to your dreams and nightmares can offer insights into your subconscious and the hidden aspects of your psyche. Recurring themes or symbols in your dreams may indicate unresolved issues that can be explored through shadow work.

-**Challenges in Relationships:** If you struggle with maintaining healthy and fulfilling relationships or have a history of difficult relationships, shadow work can help you uncover the underlying dynamics and patterns that contribute to these challenges.

-**Spiritual and Existential Questions:** If you have deep spiritual or existential questions about the nature of your soul, life's purpose, or the interconnectedness of all things, shadow work can be a path to explore these profound questions within the context of your own inner landscape.

-**Intuition and Inner Guidance:** If you have a strong inner knowing or intuition that you need to explore your hidden aspects and inner depths, this can be a compelling reason to engage in shadow work. Trusting your inner guidance can lead you on a ground-breaking adventure.

It's important to approach your shadow work with an open heart and a willingness to confront challenging aspects of yourself. While it can be a deeply rewarding process, it may also be emotionally demanding at times. If you are unsure about whether you need to do shadow work or how to begin, you may consider seeking the guidance of a therapist, counselor, or experienced practitioner who can provide support and assistance in your journey of self-discovery and healing.

6. What's the best time to start witches shadow work?

The best time to start witches shadow work can vary depending on personal preferences, magical traditions, and individual beliefs. There is no universally "best" time, but some moments and considerations may be more auspicious or significant for when you could start. Here are a few factors to keep in mind:

-Personal Readiness: The most important factor in determining when to start shadow work is your own readiness and willingness to engage in the process. Shadow work can be emotionally taxing, and you should only begin when you feel prepared to confront and address the hidden aspects of your soul.

-New Moon: You may find the new moon to be an auspicious time for new beginnings, setting intentions, and starting new projects. The energy of the new moon is often associated with fresh starts, making it a popular choice for initiating shadow work.

-Witchcraft Anniversaries: You might choose to start shadow work on anniversaries that hold personal significance in their witchcraft journey. This could be the anniversary of your initiation into a coven, a dedication to your magical practice, or a significant life event that aligns with your magical path.

-Seasonal Cycles: In some magical traditions, the seasonal cycles play a role in determining when to begin various practices, including shadow work. For example, the equinoxes and solstices may be seen as suitable times for you to begin on cathartic inner work.

-Moon Phases: Besides the new moon, other moon phases, such as the dark moon (the period just before the new moon when the moon is not visible), are also considered conducive for shadow work. The dark moon represents the hidden, introspective, and shadowy aspects, making it a fitting time for you to begin this work.

-Guidance from Spiritual Practices: You may receive guidance from your chosen spiritual path or deities regarding when to initiate shadow work. This guidance can come through dreams, divination, or direct spiritual experiences.

-Support System: Consider your support system when starting shadow work. If you have access to mentors, experienced practitioners, or a supportive community, it may be advantageous to begin when you have access to guidance and assistance.

-Consistency: Consistency in your magical and spiritual practices can also play a role in when you begin shadow work. If you have established a regular routine of meditation, ritual, or other practices, you may find it easier to incorporate shadow work into your existing framework.

Ultimately, the decision of when to start witches shadow work is a personal one, and it should be based on your own feelings, intuition, and circumstances. It's essential to approach this inner work with patience and self-compassion, as it can be a long and challenging journey. Regardless of when you begin, the most important thing is your commitment to self-awareness, healing, and personal growth.

7. Is witch's shadow work dangerous or malevolent magic?

Witch's shadow work is deeply introspective, with breakthrough practices that focus on self-exploration, healing, and self-realization. Here are some points to clarify why witch's shadow work is **not** malicious or harmful:

-**Personal Fulfillment and Recovery:** Witches shadow work is primarily about exploring your hidden aspects, such as repressed emotions, unresolved traumas, and unacknowledged fears. It is a therapeutic and cathartic process aimed at understanding and healing these aspects to achieve personal growth and emotional well-being.

-**Alignment with Psychological Concepts:** The concept of the shadow, which is central to shadow work, was popularized by Swiss psychiatrist Carl Jung. Jungian psychology acknowledges the importance of integrating the shadow for mental and emotional health. Witches shadow work draws upon these psychological insights in a spiritual and magical context.

-**Not "Dark" or "Evil":** Witches shadow work is not "dark" in the sense of being malevolent or harmful. It does not involve harmful intentions, curses, or malicious actions. Instead, it aims to promote self-awareness and positive personal transformation. The use of "dark" or "black" to describe malicious magic is problematic due to its historical associations with racial stereotypes and prejudices. In many cultural contexts, these terms have been used to portray people of color as evil or malevolent, perpetuating dangerous stereotypes. To avoid perpetuating racial connotations and promote inclusivity, many practitioners of magic and scholars of the occult now opt for alternative terminology when discussing practices with harmful or malevolent intentions.

-**Positive Intentions:** Practitioners of witches shadow work typically approach it with positive intentions, such as self-improvement, emotional healing, and spiritual growth. The work involves facing and addressing one's own inner conflicts and negative patterns in order to create a more balanced and integrated self.

-**Emotional Intensity:** Witches shadow work can be emotionally intense, as it involves you searching into challenging and often painful emotions. However, this emotional intensity is a natural part of the healing process, and it is not indicative of malevolent intent.

-**Empowerment and Personal Growth:** Witches shadow work is ultimately about your empowerment and personal growth. By confronting and integrating your shadow, you can become more self-aware, emotionally resilient, and spiritually evolved. It is a path to greater self-empowerment, not an attempt to harm others.

-**Consent and Ethics:** Be sure when practicing witches shadow work to prioritize the principle of consent. Do not seek to uncover or manipulate the shadows of others without permission, respect the boundaries of individual privacy and autonomy.

Distinguishing witch's shadow work from practices linked to baneful magic is crucial. The latter may involve harmful intentions, curses, or manipulative actions with the aim of causing harm to others. In contrast, witches shadow work centers on the self and helps you begin on an internal journey toward wholeness and self-realization.

Your transformative journey will have you jump into the depths of your psyche, presenting challenges and working through emotional intensity. However, it remains a path dedicated to self-discovery and personal development, markedly distinct from the intentions behind harmful magic. This emphasis on self-exploration underscores the ethical nature of witches shadow work, reinforcing its commitment to personal growth and inner enlightenment.

8. Can Shadow Work Address Specific Issues like Anxiety or Self-Esteem?

Yes, shadow work stands as a very effective tool for maneuvering through specific challenges such as anxiety or self-esteem issues.

-Understanding Root Causes: Search into your hidden recesses, shadow work unveils the root causes of issues like anxiety or low self-esteem. Uncovering unresolved traumas and negative beliefs becomes a crucial step toward addressing and resolving these challenges.

-Acknowledgment and Acceptance: A cornerstone principle of shadow work involves acknowledging and accepting all facets of yourself, including those contributing to anxiety or self-esteem issues. By confronting these unseen aspects without judgment, you can initiate a process of releasing the emotional burdens associated with them.

-Healing and Transformation: Once your root causes are identified and acceptance achieved, shadow work provides you a space for healing and transformation. Through this process, you can work through emotional challenges, gradually releasing their grip on mental and emotional well-being.

-Reframing Beliefs and Self-Image: Shadow work empowers you to reframe negative beliefs about yourself and your self-image. By trying and transmuting your beliefs, a healthier self-esteem can emerge, followed by a decline in anxiety. This involves replacing your self-limiting beliefs with empowering and positive narratives.

-Emotional Release: Shadow work often entails a cathartic process, releasing pent-up emotions and trauma associated with anxiety or self-esteem issues. This therapeutic release helps to lightens your emotional burden, offering relief and facilitating emotional healing.

-Increased Self-Confidence: By addressing the shadow aspects tied to self-esteem, you may experience a tangible boost in self-confidence and self-acceptance. The realization that your flaws and vulnerabilities do not define your worth becomes a revolutionary aspect of the shadow work process.

-Empowerment: Shadow work inherently aligns you with self-empowerment. Tackling specific challenges like anxiety or self-esteem issues empowers individuals to gain greater control over their emotions and responses, fostering effective coping mechanisms.

It's imperative to recognize that shadow work is a gradual process, necessitating ongoing effort and patience. Depending on the severity of specific challenges, seeking support from a therapist or counselor in conjunction with shadow work can provide a comprehensive and effective strategy for addressing these issues, ensuring a holistic approach to transformative healing.

9. Do I need to be an experienced witch to do shadow work?

You do not need to be an experienced witch or practitioner to engage in shadow work. Shadow work is a very versatile and accessible practice that can be adapted to your level of experience and understanding. Also it's not just something for witches, but for anyone who want's to learn more about themselves and to heal.

-Universal Practice: Shadow work transcends specific spiritual or magical traditions. While commonly associated with witchcraft and paganism, its fundamental concept of exploring and integrating the shadow is universal. It welcomes you to come from any belief system or experience level.

-Self-Exploration: At its essence, shadow work is a essential journey of soul-searching and discovery. It requires no specific magical skills or prior experience in witchcraft. You can root inward to confront your veiled aspects, and address unresolved issues as part of your personal growth.

-Adaptable to Personal Beliefs: Shadow work is adaptable, allowing you to align it with personal beliefs and values. Whether well-established in a belief system or still exploring spirituality, beginners can incorporate their principles into the practice.

-Access to Resources: Abundant resources cater to beginners interested in shadow work. Books, online courses, workshops, and experienced mentors offer guidance and support. These resources are designed to accommodate those new to the practice, providing a solid foundation for exploration.

-Personal Growth: A powerful tool for personal growth, shadow work aids beginners in gaining deeper self-understanding, addressing emotional challenges, and fostering self-awareness and acceptance.

-Start Small: Starting with simple techniques like meditation, journaling, and self-reflection is advisable. Building on these foundational practices gradually allows you to explore more advanced methods as you become comfortable with the process.

-Collaboration and Learning: Engaging in shadow work can be collaborative and a learning experience. Beginners can seek guidance from experienced practitioners, join supportive communities, and learn from others on the shadow work journey.

Beginners can absolutely engage in shadow work, and in fact, it can be a valuable practice for those who are new to witchcraft, spirituality, or just exploring. The key is to approach it with an open heart, a willingness to learn, and a commitment to your personal growth and healing journey. Over time, as you become more experienced and comfortable with the process, you can adapt and expand your shadow work practice to suit your evolving needs and goals.

10. How do I find my shadow self?

Exploring and confronting your shadow self is an important aspect of the tangled process of shadow work, demanding both courage and introspection:

-Self-Reflection: Initiate the process by dedicating time for you to self-reflect. Understand your thoughts, behaviors, and emotional responses, especially in situations where discomfort or recurring negative patterns arise. Inquire into the reasons behind these reactions.

-Meditation: Harness the power of meditation to burrow into the depths of your spirit. Guided meditations tailored for shadow work provide a serene mental space for you to explore hidden aspects. This practice facilitates a connection with and illumination of your concealed self.

-Journaling: Keep a shadow work journal, capturing your thoughts, emotions, dreams, and experiences tied to your self-exploration. Journaling unveils patterns and recurring themes, offering valuable insights into your shadow aspects.

-Dream Analysis: Pay mind to your dreams and nightmares, potent reflections of the subconscious mind. A dream journal aids in dissecting the symbolism and imagery, unraveling the messages emanating from your shadow self.

-Self-Observation: Observe your reactions across different life situations, particularly instances triggering an intense emotional response. Scrutinize these reactions, finding the underlying fears or unresolved issues they may expose.

-Feedback from Others: Trusted individuals, friends, family, or therapists, can provide external perspectives on your shadow self. Open yourself to constructive feedback, leveraging insights that others may discern about your hidden aspects.

-Honest Self-Examination: Embrace honest and non-judgmental self-examination. Acknowledge that shadow aspects aren't negative; they represent aspects concealed or suppressed for different reasons.

-Seek Guidance: For those new to shadow work or navigating challenging emotions, seek guidance from experienced practitioners, therapists, or mentors. Their support can help you on your path to self-discovery.

-Gradual Exploration: Uncovering your shadow self is a gradual process that demands patience and self-compassion. Avoid rushing the revelations; approach the journey with a nurturing mindset, recognizing the emotional demands it may entail.

Discovering your shadow self is a deeply personal and ongoing odyssey toward self-awareness and healing. Employing these tools and techniques allows for the gradual unveiling of hidden aspects, fostering personal growth, emotional healing, and a profound sense of wholeness.

11. Is it okay to ask for help or guidance in my shadow work?

Starting your shadow work journey is not only reasonable but also immensely advantageous when you consider the following aspects:

-Expertise and Experience: Seasoned witches, therapists, or mentors possess a wealth of expertise and experience in shadow work. Drawing from their personal journeys, they can offer profound insights, time-tested techniques, and unwavering support tailored to your unique exploration.

-Validation and Understanding: Sharing your shadow work with someone who you trust, that comprehends the process and provides validation. Discovering that your experiences and emotions are shared by others fosters a sense of unity, assuring you that similar challenges have been faced on the path to self-discovery.

-Safety and Emotional Support: The intense emotions elicited during shadow work can be challenging. Seeking emotional support and guidance ensures you navigate these moments with increased safety and ease, knowing you have a reliable source of assistance.

-Perspective: An external perspective offers fresh points of view for looking at your shadow aspects. Experienced practitioners or therapists bring a unique viewpoint to your challenges, proposing alternative approaches to resolution.

-Emotional Processing: Experienced practitioners and therapists equip you with tools and techniques to navigate the emotional processing intrinsic to shadow work. Their guidance aids in managing challenging emotions and trauma, fostering a more resilient emotional state.

-Long-Term Growth: Shadow work is an enduring process, and experienced guides assist in formulating a long-term plan for personal growth and self-awareness. They collaborate with you in setting achievable goals and milestones for your ongoing shadow work journey.

Remember, seeking help or guidance in your shadow work signifies strength and self-awareness. It's an acknowledgment of your commitment to personal growth and well-being. Whether from an experienced witch, therapist, or mentor, their support significantly enhances your shadow work experience, contributing to positive and transformative outcomes.

12. What are common challenges in witches shadow work?

-Facing Difficult Emotions: Exploring deep and sometimes painful emotions, such as fear, anger, shame, and guilt, can be emotionally challenging. Cultivating emotional resilience and self-compassion is crucial as you confront these feelings.

-Confronting Past Traumas: Witches shadow work may unveil your past traumas or unresolved issues that have been buried or avoided. Confronting these emotional intensities may necessitate a safe and supportive environment, such as therapy or guidance from experienced practitioners.

-Resistance to Change: Resistance to change, especially when challenging ingrained beliefs and behavioral patterns, is common. Overcoming this resistance requires acknowledging and addressing your fear of the unknown that often accompanies big change.

-Struggles with Self-Acceptance: Despite being centered around self-acceptance, shadow work may reveal self-criticism, self-doubt, and low self-esteem. Overcoming these challenges involves cultivating self-compassion and learning to fully accept oneself.

-Overwhelming Sensations: The intensity of shadow work may lead to overwhelming sensations like dissociation or anxiety. Approach shadow work with self-awareness and seek support when needed to manage and process these experiences.

-Dealing with Unconscious Patterns: Shadow work unveils your unconscious patterns influencing your choices and behaviors. Identifying and addressing these deeply ingrained patterns can be challenging, requiring patience and a commitment to change.

-Navigating Loneliness: The personal and introspective nature of shadow work may lead to feelings of isolation. Seeking connection and support from others who understand the intricacies of shadow work is essential during moments of loneliness.

-Integration: Integrating shadow aspects into your conscious self is an ongoing process. Living in harmony with these integrated aspects requires continuous self-reflection and self-acceptance.

-Self-Compassion: Developing self-compassion is focal in shadow work. Embracing kindness and forgiveness towards yourself, especially as you confront flaws and vulnerabilities, is an ongoing and transformative aspect of the journey.

Recognize that these challenges are inherent to the shadow work journey, offering opportunities for growth, healing, and transformation. Seeking support from experienced practitioners, therapists, or supportive communities proves invaluable in addressing these challenges and progressing on the path of witchy shadow work.

13. How do I stay safe during shadow work?

Engaging in shadow work can be emotionally and psychologically intense, make your safety a top priority. Here's a guide on how to stay safe during your shadow work journey:

-Prioritize Self-Care Practices: Make self-care a cornerstone of your shadow work. Prioritize your physical, emotional, and mental well-being by ensuring adequate rest, nourishing food, regular exercise, and stress reduction techniques.

-Set Clear Intentions: Before delving into shadow work, define clear and positive intentions. Identify your goals, what you aim to achieve, and how you envision personal growth through this process. These intentions will guide you throughout your journey.

-Seek Support: Don't hesitate to seek support when needed. Whether from a therapist, counselor, experienced practitioners, or a trusted friend, having a support system helps navigate challenges that may arise during your shadow work.

-Utilize Guided Meditation: Use guided meditations specifically designed for shadow work.(There is one created for this book listed in chapter 6.) These structured sessions provide a safe environment for exploring your inner world, offering guidance on how to work with your shadow aspects.

-Approach Rituals and Spellwork Mindfully: When incorporating rituals and spellwork, maintain clear and positive intentions. Use these practices as tools for healing and transformation, avoiding manipulation or control. Be mindful of ethical considerations. (Chapter 4 has a spell and Chapter 7 has a ritual.)

-Establish Healthy Boundaries: Set boundaries for your shadow work, including limits on intensity and duration. Respect your emotional boundaries, and if emotions become overwhelming, step back and seek support or professional help. (Chapter 4 has a boundary spell)

-Keep a Shadow Work Journal: Document your experiences and insights in a shadow work journal. It aids in processing emotions, tracking progress, and gaining clarity about your shadow aspects, offering a safe outlet for self-expression.

-Regular Self-Reflection: Engage in regular self-reflection. Check in with yourself to assess emotional well-being. If you notice signs of emotional distress, difficulty managing emotions, or other challenges, reach out for assistance.

-Empowerment and Consent: Ensure your shadow work is empowering and consensual. Do not explore or manipulate others' shadows without permission, and respect your own boundaries and consent throughout the process.

-Create a Safe Space: Establish a safe and sacred space for your shadow work, be it a physical area, an altar, or a designated practice space. This space should feel protective and supportive, allowing you to focus on your inner work.

-Incorporate Grounding Techniques: Integrate grounding techniques into your shadow work. These methods help anchor you in the present moment, assisting in managing any overwhelming or disorienting experiences that may arise.

-Practice Ongoing Self-Compassion: Embrace self-compassion throughout your shadow work journey. Extend kindness, understanding, and forgiveness to yourself as you confront inner challenges and vulnerabilities.

-Consider Therapeutic Integration: If your shadow work reveals deep-seated emotional trauma or psychological issues, consider integrating therapy into your practice. A therapist can provide professional support for addressing and healing these issues.

Remember, shadow work is a hands-on journey. Approach it with self-awareness and self-care to reap the benefits of self-discovery and healing while effectively managing any challenges that may arise.

14. Can I do shadow work for someone else, like a friend or family member?

Engaging in shadow work is a profoundly personal and introspective journey, and it remains exclusive to the individual undertaking it. Here's an explanation of why shadow work cannot be conducted on behalf of someone else and the importance of autonomy:

-Personal Nature of Shadow Work: Shadow work is an exploration of your own spirit, emotions, and experiences. Its depth is uniquely tailored to each individual, making it impossible for someone else to navigate the intricacies of another person's inner world.

-Autonomy and Self-Discovery: True shadow work necessitates an individual to take ownership of their internal processes. It's a journey of self-awareness, healing, and personal growth that cannot be outsourced or delegated to another person.

-Respect for Boundaries: Shadow work often involves sensitive and potentially painful emotions. Respecting emotional boundaries and obtaining consent is crucial. Attempting to conduct shadow work for someone else without their consent can be intrusive and counterproductive.

-Empowerment and Responsibility: Shadow work empowers you to confront and transform your own shadows. It fosters self-responsibility and self-empowerment, both vital for personal growth. This journey is an inherently individual process.

-Support and Guidance: While you cannot perform shadow work on someone else's behalf, you can offer support and guidance if they decide to embark on their journey. Be a listening ear, provide resources, and share your experiences, respecting their autonomy and decisions.

-Group or Shared Experiences: Some shadow work practices involve group activities or shared experiences. Even in these cases, participants voluntarily contribute their individual perspectives and experiences to collective explorations.

-Therapy: For individuals grappling with severe emotional trauma or psychological issues, seeking professional therapeutic guidance from a trained therapist or counselor may be appropriate. Therapists can help navigate shadow aspects in a therapeutic and safe context.

It's crucial to respect the personal and autonomous nature of shadow work, encouraging others to engage in their self-exploration if they choose to do so. While you can provide support, encouragement, and resources, each person's journey through shadow work is a deeply individual and transformative experience that cannot be undertaken by someone else.

15. How long does witch's shadow work typically take?

Beginning the journey of witch's shadow work is a unique and individual experience, and the timeline for this process is highly variable. Some of these factors can influence the duration of your witch's shadow work:

-Complexity of Shadow Aspects: The intricacy and depth of your shadow aspects significantly impact the duration of your shadow work. Some may have more straightforward aspects, allowing for quicker exploration, while others with deeply ingrained or multifaceted issues may require more time.

-Commitment and Consistency: Your commitment and consistency in engaging with shadow work play a large role. While frequent and consistent involvement can expedite progress, rushing through the process is discouraged, as it may hinder rather than aid your journey.

-Emotional Readiness: Emotional readiness and the willingness to confront shadow aspects are key. Taking the time you need to emotionally prepare for the challenges of shadow work is crucial, ensuring a more sustainable and effective process.

-Therapeutic Integration: If your shadow work unveils deep-seated trauma or psychological issues, integrating therapy or counseling into your journey may extend the timeline. While it may elongate the process, this support is often essential for profound healing.

-Self-Reflection: Shadow work isn't a one-time event; it's a continual process of self-reflection and integration. Even after initial phases, ongoing exploration and integration of new shadow aspects may continue to unfold in various life situations.

-Support and Guidance: Experienced guides, mentors, or supportive communities can expedite your comprehension of shadow work concepts, potentially accelerating the time it takes to grasp key insights and navigate your personal journey.

-Customized Goals: Your individual goals and intentions for shadow work will vary. Whether focusing on specific issues or taking a more comprehensive approach, the depth and breadth of your goals influence the overall timeline of your journey.

-Spiritual and Magical Practices: Witch's shadow work can be intertwined with spiritual and magical practices, often following lunar or seasonal cycles. The timing of shadow work sessions may align with these practices, influencing the overall duration.

-Balance with Daily Life: Balancing shadow work with daily responsibilities impacts the pace of your engagement. The time and energy you allocate alongside your everyday life commitments contribute to the overall rhythm of your shadow work.

Remember, approaching witch's shadow work with patience and self-compassion is essential. There's no prescribed timeline for this journey, and it's not a race. Embrace the ongoing process of self-awareness, healing, and personal growth, allowing the transformation to unfold at a pace that resonates with your unique experience.

16. Can I stop shadow work once I start, or is it ongoing?

-Continuous Self-Discovery: The essence of shadow work lies in perpetual self-discovery. As long as you're alive and evolving, there will be new layers of the self to explore, comprehend, and integrate.

-Unveiling Deeper Layers: Progressing in shadow work initially addresses surface-level aspects. Yet, with continued engagement, deeper layers of your heart may reveal themselves, demanding attention and healing.

-Life Changes and Challenges: Life events introduce new shadow aspects or reawaken old ones. Major transitions, relationships, career shifts, or personal crises prompt the revisiting and reevaluation of your shadow work.

-Self-Reflection and Healing: Shadow work offers a platform for regular self-reflection and emotional healing, maintaining emotional and psychological well-being. It becomes a tool to address emerging issues and challenges.

-Breaks and Rest: Taking breaks from intense shadow work is acceptable and crucial for emotional well-being. Even during these respites, the process of self-reflection and growth can persist, albeit in a more relaxed manner.

-Support and Guidance: Ongoing support from mentors, therapists, or experienced practitioners remains valuable. These guides offer insights and tools, aiding your navigation of the continuous process effectively.

-Ritual and Spiritual Practices: Many integrate shadow work into spiritual and magical practices, aligning it with lunar or seasonal cycles. These practices structure and time your ongoing engagement with shadow work.

While breaks from intense shadow work are healthy, the journey of self-discovery and personal growth remains ceaseless. Embrace shadow work as a lifelong expedition, receptive to transformation and growth at every stage of your life. The unending path offers profound insights and continuous evolution, marking each step with the promise of greater self-awareness and wholeness.

17. What should I do if I encounter resistance or fear during shadow work?

Encountering resistance or fear during your shadow work is a natural facet of the process. Here's some help for you to navigate these challenging emotions:

-Acknowledge Your Feelings: The first step is to acknowledge your emotions without judgment. Recognize that these feelings are a natural response to the profound self-exploration inherent in shadow work.

-Take a Step Back: If you're overwhelmed, it's entirely appropriate to step back from your shadow work. Allow yourself time and space to process emotions. Resume the work when you feel more emotionally ready.

-Self-Compassion: Practice self-compassion. Be kind and gentle with yourself, understanding that shadow work is a process, and it's okay to experience difficult emotions. Self-compassion alleviates emotional burden.

-Seek Support: Don't hesitate to seek support from a therapist, counselor, mentor, or a trusted friend. Professional guidance can help work through fears and resistance in a safe, structured manner. Sharing experiences provides emotional relief.

-Grounding Techniques: Utilize grounding techniques—deep breathing, mindfulness, or meditation—to stay rooted in the present and manage overwhelming emotions when fear or resistance arises.

-Identify the Source: Reflect on the source of resistance or fear. Are specific memories, experiences, or beliefs triggering these emotions? Identifying the source brings clarity and guides the healing process.

-Break Down the Work: If fear or resistance is linked to specific shadow aspects, break down the work into manageable steps. Tackling one aspect at a time makes the process less overwhelming.

-Positive Affirmations: Incorporate positive affirmations into your practice. They reframe negative beliefs, offering emotional support as you navigate your shadow aspects.

-Emotional Release: Allow yourself to experience and release deep-seated emotions in a safe environment, through journaling, art, or therapeutic techniques, if resistance and fear signal the surfacing of buried emotions.

-Energetic Protection: Utilize energetic protection techniques, like creating a protective energy shield or using specific crystals or talismans, to enhance the sense of safety during shadow work.

Remember, encountering resistance or fear is a natural part of your shadow work journey, indicating the potential for deep insights and healing opportunities. By acknowledging emotions, seeking support, practicing self-compassion, and approaching your shadow work with patience, you can effectively navigate these challenges and continue your path of self-discovery and growth.

18. What are some signs of progress in shadow work?

-Increased Self-Awareness: Heightened self-awareness is a significant indicator of progress. Through delving into your inner world, you gain clarity on thoughts, emotions, behaviors, and patterns. This awareness empowers you to make more informed choices.

-Improved Emotional Well-Being: Shadow work often results in improved emotional well-being. By confronting and addressing unresolved emotional issues, you experience emotional healing and a greater sense of stability. Managing and regulating your emotions becomes more attainable.

-Resolution of Past Trauma: Progress may manifest as the resolution of past traumas or emotional wounds. With greater peace and closure, you can revisit and heal painful memories.

-Release of Repressed Emotions: Shadow work allows the release of repressed emotions, leading to emotional catharsis. Allowing these emotions to surface provides a sense of relief and emotional lightness.

-Empowerment: A growing sense of personal empowerment is a significant sign of progress. Confronting and integrating your shadow aspects into your conscious self reveals your transformative capacity and the ability to make choices aligned with your true self.

-Improved Relationships: Progress positively impacts relationships with improved communication, empathy, and understanding. Heightened self-awareness allows you to relate to others authentically.

-Balanced Sense of Self: Achieving a balanced sense of self is another indicator of progress. Embracing and integrating both light and dark aspects contributes to a healthier self-esteem.

-Clarity on Life Goals: Working through shadow aspects provides clarity on life goals, values, and priorities. Aligning actions and decisions with your authentic self becomes more attainable.

-Reduced Self-Sabotage: Progress results in a reduction of self-sabotaging behaviors. Increased consciousness of destructive patterns equips you to interrupt them before undermining your well-being.

-Spiritual and Magical Growth: For those integrating shadow work into spiritual or magical practices, signs include heightened insight, improved magical abilities, and a stronger connection to spiritual or divine forces.

-Sense of Wholeness: Ultimately, a profound sign of progress is a sense of wholeness and integration. Acceptance of all aspects of your being leads to feeling complete and at ease with yourself.

-Liberation from Limiting Beliefs: Progress often entails liberation from limiting beliefs. Shedding outdated and self-defeating beliefs opens doors to new opportunities and personal growth.

-Greater Resilience: Navigating and addressing challenging emotions fosters greater emotional resilience. The ability to cope with life's ups and downs becomes a testament to your growth.

19. Can shadow work be integrated into everyday life and rituals?

-Daily Self-Reflection: Make self-reflection a daily habit. Dedicate a few moments each day to checking in with yourself, exploring your emotions and thoughts. This consistent practice builds self-awareness and provides continual opportunities for shadow work.

-Journaling: Maintain a shadow work journal where you document thoughts, emotions, and experiences related to your inner exploration. Regular journaling helps track your progress, revealing recurring patterns that may signify your shadow aspects.

-**Meditation:** Incorporate daily or regular meditation sessions into your routine. Meditation serves as a valuable tool for connecting with your inner self, exploring your subconscious, and addressing shadow aspects. Guided meditations tailored for shadow work can be particularly beneficial.

-**Rituals:** Create specific rituals for shadow work, integrating them into your routine, such as during the new moon or other significant times in your spiritual practice. These rituals may involve candle magic, crystal work, and visualization techniques aimed at exploring and addressing your shadow aspects.

-**Spellwork:** Craft spells aligned with your shadow work goals. Focus on personal transformation, emotional healing, or empowerment. By weaving shadow work intentions into your spellwork, you align your magical practice with your inner journey.

-**Daily Affirmations:** Use daily affirmations that reinforce positive self-concepts and self-acceptance. These affirmations counteract negative beliefs and self-criticism often encountered in shadow work.

-**Tarot or Oracle Cards:** Incorporate tarot or oracle cards into your daily divination practice. Utilize them to gain insights into your shadow aspects and receive guidance on how to address them.

- **Shadow Altar:** Create a shadow altar as a dedicated space for your shadow work. Place objects, symbols, and representations of your shadow aspects on this altar, making it a focal point for your daily practice.

-**Dream Work:** Pay attention to your dreams and nightmares. Keep a dream journal to record your experiences. Dreams often provide valuable symbolism and insights into your subconscious, including shadow aspects.

-**Affirm Shadow Integration:** Regularly affirm your commitment to shadow integration as part of your daily magical practice. This conscious intention keeps you focused on your self-discovery and healing journey.

-**Continual Learning:** Continuously educate yourself about shadow work concepts, techniques, and resources. Read books, articles, and attend workshops related to shadow work to deepen your understanding and refine your practice.

-**Seek Support:** Consider joining or forming a shadow work group or community. Engage with like-minded individuals who are also integrating shadow work into their daily lives, providing support and shared experiences.

-Ongoing Transformation: Embrace shadow work as an ongoing transformational process. Understand that it is not a one-time task but a lifelong journey of self-awareness, healing, and personal growth.

20. Can witches shadow work be combined with other spiritual or religious practices?

At the starting poing of integration into witch's shadow work with other spiritual or religious practices is a profound and personal journey. Here's a comprehensive guide to help you navigate and harmonize these diverse elements within your spiritual framework:

-Respect for Diversity: Embrace an attitude of respect for diversity. Acknowledge that individuals come from various spiritual backgrounds, each with unique beliefs and practices. Foster an open and inclusive environment that honors different paths.

-Common Elements: Recognize common elements shared among various spiritual and religious traditions and witch's shadow work. These commonalities often center around self-exploration, healing, and personal growth. Identify these shared aspects to find points of connection and integration.

-Adaptation and Customization: Tailor your approach to shadow work to align with the specific beliefs and practices of your spiritual or religious path. Customize the terminology, symbols, and rituals to harmonize seamlessly with your existing spiritual framework.

-Ritual Integration: Infuse shadow work into your spiritual or religious rituals and ceremonies. For instance, during meditation or prayer, focus on exploring and addressing your shadow aspects, seeking guidance, or finding healing through your spiritual practice.

-Ceremonial Magic: If you engage in ceremonial magic, incorporate shadow work as a foundational step in your magical operations. Use it to purify and cleanse your inner self, creating a suitable vessel for magical work.

-Divination: Combine divination practices with shadow work. Employ tools like tarot cards or runes to gain insights into your shadow aspects and receive guidance on how to navigate and integrate them effectively.

-Spiritual Guidance: Seek guidance from spiritual or religious leaders well-versed in your specific path. They can offer insights and recommendations on how to seamlessly integrate shadow work within the context of your beliefs.

-Healing and Forgiveness: Leverage the healing and forgiveness principles present in many religious traditions. Utilize your spiritual or religious practices to facilitate the healing process as you navigate and address your shadow aspects.

-Syncretism: If inclined, embrace syncretism by blending elements from different spiritual or religious traditions. This personalized approach can lead to a unique path that authentically integrates witch's shadow work with other practices.

-Closed Practices Consideration: Be cautious when blending closed practices. Closed practices involve cultural, ethnic, or historical roots and are reserved only for those deeply connected to that culture or community. Respect the boundaries and sacredness of closed practices.

-Respect for Cultural Appropriation: Understand the concept of cultural appropriation and avoid engaging in closed practices without proper understanding, permission, or belonging to the respective cultural or spiritual community.

-Cultural Understanding: Acknowledge that closed practices hold a deep cultural and historical context. Respect the significance and meaning behind the rituals, symbols, and beliefs to avoid misunderstandings and misinterpretations.

-Maintaining Authenticity: Recognize that blending elements without a deep connection can dilute the authenticity of both practices. Strive for a blend that respects and honors the depth and significance of each tradition.

-Preventing Harm to Communities: Understand that inappropriate use of closed practices can cause harm or offense to the community that holds these traditions dear. Avoid contributing to cultural insensitivity and stereotypes.

-Spiritual Ethics: Adhere to the ethical guidelines and principles of your spiritual or religious traditions. Ensure that your integration of practices aligns with these principles, avoiding any violation of spiritual ethics.

Chapter 36

Resources for Empowerment and Well-being

Books:

1. "The Witch's Book of Shadows" by Phyllis Curott - This book provides insights into witchcraft, including the practice of shadow work, from a modern witch's perspective.

2. "Journey to the Dark Goddess: How to Return to Your Soul" by Jane Meredith - A resource that focuses on embracing the shadow and working with dark goddess archetypes.

3. "The Inner Temple of Witchcraft: Magick, Meditation, and Psychic Development" by Christopher Penczak - A guide to inner and outer work in witchcraft, including shadow work techniques.

4. "The Witch's Book of Shadows: The Craft, Lore & Magick of the Witch's Grimoire" by Phyllis Curott - This book offers a comprehensive guide to various aspects of witchcraft, including shadow work.

5. "The Dark Goddess: Dancing with the Shadow" by Marcia Starck and Gynne Stern - Explore the concept of the dark goddess and how it relates to shadow work in this enlightening book.

6. "Witchcraft and Mental Health: An Anthology" by Mandi See - This book delves into the connection between witchcraft and mental health, with contributions from various authors sharing their experiences and insights.

7. "The Witch's Book of Shadows: The Craft, Lore & Magick of the Witch's Grimoire" by Phyllis Curott - While not solely focused on mental health, this book offers guidance on holistic well-being within a witchcraft context.

8. "Tarot for Your Self: A Workbook for Personal Transformation" by Mary K. Greer - This book combines tarot, self-discovery, and mental health, offering a unique approach to understanding and healing the self.

Websites and Online Resources:

1. **Witchvox (www.witchvox.com)** - Witchvox offers a wide range of articles and resources on various aspects of witchcraft, including shadow work.

2. **The Witch of Lupine Hollow (www.thewitchoflupinehollow.com)** - A blog and website dedicated to witchcraft, spirituality, and shadow work.

3. **The Sacred Grove (www.thesacredgrove.co.uk)** - This website offers a variety of resources and articles on witchcraft and shadow work.

4. **The Witches' Voice (www.witchesvoice.com)** - An extensive online community and resource hub for witches and pagans, including articles on shadow work.

5. **The Green Witchcraft Blog (www.greenwitchcraft.com)** - A blog dedicated to green witchcraft and related topics, including shadow work.

6. **The Witch of Lupine Hollow (www.thewitchoflupinehollow.com)** - A blog dedicated to the intersection of witchcraft and mental health, offering resources, articles, and personal experiences.

7. **The Hoodwitch (www.thehoodwitch.com)** - While primarily a resource for all things witchy, this website often touches on self-care, healing, and mental well-being within the context of witchcraft.

8. **"The Witches' Voice" (www.witchesvoice.com)** - An extensive online community and resource hub for witches and pagans that may have articles and discussions on witchy mental health.

Online Communities:

Witchy Forums, Groups and Subreddits - Online forums, such as r/witchcraft on Reddit or witchy communities on platforms like Tumblr and Pinterest, offer great opportunities to connect with others engaged in shadow work. Additionally, Reddit hosts various subreddits like r/witchcraft, r/pagan, and r/mentalhealth, where individuals discuss the intersection of witchcraft and mental health, providing valuable resources and supportive communities.

www.ingramcontent.com/pod-product-compliance
Lightning Source LLC
Chambersburg PA
CBHW081211130726
47997CB00009B/2623